# How to
# STUDY
## the
# BIBLE

WATCHMAN NEE

**Living Stream Ministry**
Anaheim, California • www.lsm.org

First Edition, February 1999.

ISBN 0-7363-0407-X

Published by

*Living Stream Ministry*
2431 W. La Palma Ave., Anaheim, CA 92801 U.S.A.
P. O. Box 2121, Anaheim, CA 92814 U.S.A.

*Printed in the United States of America*

99  00  01  02  03  04  05  /  11  10  9  8  7  6  5  4  3  2

# CONTENTS

# PREFACE

This book, *How to Study the Bible,* contains messages given by Watchman Nee in Kuling during his training for his co-workers between 1948 and 1949.

## PREFACE TO THE CHINESE EDITION

The Bible is the inspired word of God, and every child of God should spend time to study it.

The Bible shows us what God has done for us in the past and what He has said. It also shows us the ways that God has guided men in the past. In order to acquaint ourselves with the riches and vastness of God's provisions, we have to study the Bible.

God's present speaking is based on His past speaking. When God speaks to others through us, He does so through His established word. We must let the word of God dwell richly in our hearts before we can hear His speaking today and before He can make us ministers of His word.

The purpose in publishing these messages is to provide the readers with the prerequisites to the study of the Bible and to furnish them with some important tools in the study of the Word. It is our hope to render some help to those who have a desire to know the Scripture. May God bless this book and its readers.

Taiwan Gospel Book Room

# SECTION ONE

# PREPARING THE PERSON

# INTRODUCTION

In order to study the Bible properly, one has to meet two basic requirements. The first requirement is that the person must be right; he must pass through proper training. The second requirement is that he has to have the right methods. During the past few centuries, in particular since the rise of Protestantism, many books have been published on the study of the Bible. Many of them are very good, but almost all are short in one matter—they only pay attention to methods of studying the Bible; they do not pay enough attention to the person who is studying the Bible. They give the impression that anyone who uses these methods will achieve good results. Many have tried these methods but have not found any profit to their study. Those who have written books on the study of the Scripture have studied the Scripture well, but those who try to imitate them by approaching the Bible with the same methods do not necessarily fare as well. This is because the imitators have forgotten who they are. The study of the Bible is not only a matter of methods but a matter of the person. Some study the Bible well because they—the persons—have learned the proper lessons from God. When they find the right methods to assist in their study, they reap rich results. It is wrong to pass on methods without considering the kind of person one has to be. Even when some have the right methods, they can never study the Bible well because they are wrong in their very person.

This is a very important point. The study of the Bible is not merely a matter of right methods but a matter of right persons. A person must be right before he can adopt the right method to study the Bible. Methods are important because without good methods, one cannot study the Bible well. But the person must also be properly calibrated before he can study the Bible well. Some people have a misguided concept that very few people can study the Bible. Others have a mistaken notion that anyone can study the Bible. Both are wrong. It is wrong to think that very few people can study the Bible, and it is equally wrong to think that everyone can study the Bible. Only one kind of person can study the Bible, and we have to be that kind of person before we can study the Bible well. We have to see that the person is first; the methods second. If the person is wrong, nothing will work even if one has all the right methods. If the person is right, the right methods can be put to good use. Some people pay much attention to good methods. Even though we also pay proper attention to good methods, we should never make methods our first priority. *The methods do not come first; the person does.* First, we have to be right in our person, and then we can speak about the best methods of Bible study.

In order to answer the question on how to study the Bible, we have divided our discussion into two parts. The first part concerns the preparation of the person, and the second part concerns the methods of studying. We will first consider the preparation of the person.

# CHAPTER ONE

# THREE PREREQUISITES

## I. THE NEED TO BE SPIRITUAL

### A. "The Words Which I Have Spoken...Are Spirit"

In John 6:63 the Lord Jesus said, "The words which I have spoken to you are spirit." The words of the Bible are not only letters but spirit. We also should recall the Lord's word in John 4:24: "God is Spirit, and those who worship Him must worship in spirit." Here the Lord points out a fundamental principle: God is Spirit, and man can only touch Him with his spirit. God is Spirit, and we can only worship Him with our spirit; we cannot worship Him with anything other than the spirit. God is Spirit, and we cannot worship Him with our mind, emotion, or will. Colossians 2:23 speaks of "self-imposed worship." This means worshipping with the will. This is wrong because God is Spirit, and because God is Spirit, those who worship Him must worship in spirit. John 6 says that the Lord's words are spirit. The basic principle is the same: Since the Lord's words are spirit, we have to read them in spirit. In other words, we can only touch spiritual things with the spirit.

The Bible is not only a book with words or letters printed on pages of paper. The very nature of the Bible is spirit. For this reason, everyone who reads this book must approach it *with his spirit;* it must be read *with the spirit.* The spirit that we are referring to is the spirit of every regenerated person. We call this spirit the "regenerated spirit." Not everyone has this spirit. Therefore, not everyone can read the Bible well. Only those who have this spirit can read the Bible well; those who do not have this spirit cannot read it well. This spirit is needed to worship God. This same spirit is needed to read the Bible well. Without this spirit, a man cannot know God.

Without this spirit, he cannot know the Bible either. Perhaps we were born into a Christian family. Before we were regenerated, we probably had read the Bible already, but we did not understand it. We understood the history and facts recorded in the Bible, but we did not understand the Bible itself. This is not surprising, because God's word is spirit. If we do not use our spirit, we cannot read this book. When can a man begin to understand the Bible? On the day he receives the Lord, he can begin to understand the Bible. From that day forward, the Bible will become a new book to him; he will begin to understand and treasure this book. Although he may not understand everything in it, he will begin to love it. He will read it daily and yearly. If he misses his reading, he will feel hungry; he will feel that something is missing in his life. When he reads God's word this way, he will begin to understand it. He can understand it because he is now regenerated. "That which is born of the Spirit is spirit" (John 3:6). We should put John 4:24, 6:63, and 3:6 together: "God is Spirit," "The words which I have spoken...are spirit," and "That which is born of the Spirit is spirit." The words in the Bible are spirit. The life which a man receives at the time of regeneration is spirit, and it takes a man with a spirit to read the words of spirit. Only then will the Bible shine within him, and only then will it become useful to him.

No matter how clever and well educated a man is, as long as he is not regenerated, this book is a mystery to him. A regenerated person may not be that cultivated, but he is more qualified to read the Bible than an unregenerated college professor. The former has a regenerated spirit, while the latter does not have such a spirit. The Bible is not understood by talent, research, or intelligence. Since God's word is spirit, only a man with a regenerated spirit can understand it. *The root, the very nature, of the Bible is spiritual.* If a man does not have a regenerated spirit, he cannot understand this book; it will be a closed book to him.

The Lord Jesus said in John 6:55, "My flesh is true food, and My blood is true drink." The unbelieving Jews were shocked at such a word. How could the Lord's flesh be food and His blood be drink? Yet every regenerated person knows

THREE PREREQUISITES

11

that this refers to the Son of God. He bows his head and confesses, "I derive my life from Your flesh and Your blood. Without Your flesh, I will not have life today. Without Your blood, I cannot live today. You are indeed my food." A man with a regenerated spirit will not be bothered by the Lord's word but will thank and praise Him instead.

The Lord said, "It is the Spirit who gives life; the flesh profits nothing; the words which I have spoken to you are spirit and are life" (v. 63). Here we see two realms. One is the realm of spirit, the other is the realm of flesh. In the realm of spirit, everything is living and profitable. In the realm of flesh, everything is unprofitable. One must read the Bible with his spirit and in the realm of spirit. No matter how educated, logical, and analytical a man is, he cannot understand the Bible if he does not have this spirit.

God is Spirit. We know God today because we have a spirit. When some unbelievers argue with us, we may not match them in eloquence or wisdom, and we may not be able to tell them profound teachings, but we have the confidence that we know God because we are regenerated. We have a regenerated spirit, and we can touch God with this spirit. It does not matter if we can relate the doctrine or not. The fact is that we have touched God. Unbelievers want to find out about God through analysis, synthesis, and reasoning. But even when the analysis, synthesis, and reasoning are all well founded, they will still not believe in God, because God can never be analyzed or synthesized. Job said, "Can you find out the depths of God?" (Job 11:7). No one can find out God by research. There is only one way to find out God—by the regenerated spirit. Those who touch God with this spirit will know Him right away. There is no other way except this way. In order to study the Bible, a man must have a regenerated spirit, in the same way that he must have a regenerated spirit to touch God. Suppose a man has installed an electric lamp in his house. He wants to connect the lamp to the power source, but the only materials he has are wood, bamboo, and cloth; he does not have any copper wire. Although there is power in the electric power company, that power cannot cause the lamp to shine. No matter how much cloth, bamboo, and wood he has, he cannot tap into the electricity. Another man may not have any cloth, bamboo, or wood, but he has a little piece of wire. With that little wire he can light up the lamp because the wire transmits electricity. In the same way, a man must have a regenerated spirit before he can touch God. He must have a regenerated spirit before he can touch God's word.

Only one part within our whole being can study the Bible—our regenerated spirit. If we use any other part of our being to touch the Bible, we are doing something apart from God, and such activity will not touch anything related to Him. The Bible can either be a matter of flesh to man or a matter of spirit to him. If a man does not have a regenerated spirit, and if all he has is the flesh and things related to the flesh, the Bible will be a matter of flesh to him. If a man has a regenerated spirit, and such a spirit is functional within him, he will touch the spirit when he touches God's word. This is not to say that the Bible can become something other than spirit. The Bible itself is always spirit. The Lord Jesus said, "It is the Spirit who gives life; the flesh profits nothing; the words which I have spoken to you are spirit and are life." The Lord's words are spirit. Yet they are spirit only to the believers who have believed into Him; to the unbelieving Jews His words were received as a matter of flesh. The way many people study the Bible is outrageous. The reason they do this is that they are lacking the spirit. A man cannot study God's Word according to his own mind or intelligence. He must have this spirit before he can study God's word.

### B. "Interpreting Spiritual Things to Spiritual Men"

Some may ask, "I am regenerated, and I have a regenerated spirit. But why can I not study the Bible well? Why is the Bible like a closed book to me?" In order to answer this question, we should turn to one passage in the Scriptures— 1 Corinthians 2. First let us read verses 1 to 4: "And I, when I came to you, brothers, came not according to excellence of speech or of wisdom, announcing to you the mystery of God. For I did not determine to know anything among you except Jesus Christ, and this One crucified. And I was with you in weakness and in fear and in much trembling; and my speech and my proclamation were not in persuasive words of wisdom but in demonstration of the Spirit and of power." The subject of this chapter is Paul's preaching being not with persuasive words of wisdom. Read also verses 5 to 7: "In order that your faith would not stand in the wisdom of men but in the power of God. But we do speak wisdom among those who are full-grown, yet a wisdom not of this age...But we speak God's wisdom in a mystery, the wisdom which has been hidden, which God predestined before the ages for our glory." Read also verses 9 to 13: "'Things which eye has not seen and ear has not heard and which have not come up in man's heart; things which God has prepared for those who love Him.' But to us God has revealed them through the Spirit, for the Spirit searches all things, even the depths of God. For who among men knows the things of man, except the spirit of man which is in him? In the same way, the things of God also no one has known except the Spirit of God. But we have received not the spirit of the world but the Spirit which is from God, that we may know the things which have been graciously given to us by God; which things also we speak, not in words taught by human wisdom but in words taught by the Spirit, interpreting spiritual things with spiritual words." In the margin of the American Standard Version we find the alternate translation for the last part of verse 13: "Interpreting spiritual things to spiritual men." This is a better translation of the original language. The subject of chapter three is the different kinds of persons. Therefore, the end of chapter two cannot be speaking of things. It is contrary to the rule of interpretation to explain a word in two different ways within the same passage. Paul was saying that spiritual things can only be communicated to spiritual men. (The word *interpreting* in Greek can mean joining together, mingling together, or coordinated together. Therefore, it can be translated as "communicating"—communicating spiritual things to spiritual men.)

In reading this passage, we find the relationship between the spirit and the Bible. Paul was speaking here about words revealed by the Spirit, taught by the Spirit, and words of wisdom from the Spirit, not words of wisdom from men. What are words of wisdom from men? What the eyes see, what the ears hear, and what comes up in the heart—these are men's words. Where was Paul's revelation coming from? His revelation came from the Holy Spirit, because only the Holy Spirit knows the things of God. How can men have this revelation from the Holy Spirit? Paul told us that in order to have this, there is the need to have the Spirit of God. This is identical to what we saw earlier from the Gospel of John. Here it says that no one has known the things of God except the Spirit of God. It follows, therefore, that anyone who does not have the Spirit of God does not know the things of God. Paul further stated that he did not speak these things according to excellence of speech or of wisdom, nor in words taught by human wisdom, but in words taught by the Spirit, communicating spiritual things to spiritual men.

Here Paul said that spiritual things can only be communicated to spiritual men. It is impossible to communicate some things to some people; such things are not compatible with these people. Verse 14 says, "But a soulish man does not receive the things of the Spirit of God." Not only will the soulish man not receive the spiritual things, but "they are foolishness to him." He will think that believers are fools. A soulish man will not know, "and he is not able to know them because they are discerned spiritually." This word touches the peak of this passage. It shows us that spiritual things can only be discerned by spiritual men. A soulish man cannot discern these things and does not know anything about them. This has nothing to do with spending time or not spending time in the exercise. Even if a soulish man spends all his time in discerning, he cannot and will not know these things. He is short of one vital faculty. A somewhat more scientific description of the soulish man is the psychological man, the man under the control of his own psychology. Spiritually speaking, it is the unregenerated man. A soulish man is a natural man, an unregenerated man. He is like Adam, a living soul, who does not have the Spirit of God within him and who cannot know the things of God.

As a rule, after a man becomes a Christian, he should know the things of the Spirit. But why is it that so many brothers and sisters do not know them? The reason is that though they have a regenerated spirit, they are not necessarily spiritual men. Paul's emphasis in 1 Corinthians 2 and 3 is not merely the spirit but to be spiritual. John's emphasis is the spirit, but Paul's emphasis is on being spiritual. A man must not only have the spirit but must be spiritual according to this spirit. One must have the spirit; without the spirit one can do nothing. But to have the spirit alone without living under the principle of this spirit, that is, without living in this spirit and walking according to this spirit to be a spiritual man, is useless.

Suppose you take a man who is born blind into a garden and tell him that he is standing in front of a mango tree. You can explain to the blind man what the fruits are like. But will he understand what you are saying? Even if he is very clever, very discerning, and has very sharp ears, he will still not understand what a mango tree is like. You can tell him about green, but he will not understand what green is. The world of sound is different from the world of sight, and the world of sight is different from the world of thoughts. In the same way, one has to exercise his spirit before he can realize the spiritual world. Those who have eyes may not necessarily see; one must exercise the function of the eyes before he can see. A blind man cannot see the mango tree. A man with good eyes can only see the mango tree if he opens his eyes. A blind man cannot see the mango tree with his ears. A normal man cannot see the mango tree either if he only uses his ears. The problem today is that blind ones have no eyes to see the mango tree, while men with good eyes try to hear the mango tree with their ears. A soulish man cannot know God; no one can know Him by turning to soulish faculties. But a man with a regenerated spirit does not know God either if he only uses his soul. This does not mean that anyone who has a spirit can know God. Even after God's Spirit has entered into a man, it is still possible for that man to not know God. Wisdom and intelligence do not help an unbeliever know God; neither do they help a Christian know God. Knowledge does not help an unbeliever understand the Bible; neither does it help a Christian understand the Bible. The way to understand the Bible is by the spirit. It is not merely a matter of having the spirit, but a matter of being spiritual. No one can say that he has a spirit but does not have to walk according to it and instead can walk according to his former ways. Such ways were unacceptable when the man did not have a regenerated spirit; they are equally unacceptable now that he has a regenerated spirit. The fundamental way to the understanding of the Bible is through the spirit. This is the reason Paul showed us in 1 Corinthians 2 that the issue is not having or not having the spirit, but of being spiritual or not being spiritual. Spiritual things are discerned only by spiritual men.

First Corinthians 3:1 says, "And I, brothers, was not able to speak to you as to spiritual men, but as to fleshy, as to infants in Christ." Here is another word: fleshy. The Corinthian believers were infants in Christ; they were fleshy. This is the reason verse 2 says, "I gave you milk to drink, not solid food." To be sure, such ones are not totally ignorant of spiritual things. Yet they can only touch the most obvious revelations; they cannot touch anything deeper. They are fleshy, and therefore they can only take milk, not solid food. Milk is for those in their first stage of life. This means that these ones can only take the most elemental revelations in Christianity. Solid food, on the other hand, is for a grown-up throughout his lifetime. It refers to the deeper and more profound revelations. A man does not continue drinking milk all the time; there is only a short period during his life when he has to drink milk. Yet there are men who, like the Corinthian believers, are drinking milk all the time. "For you were not yet able to receive it. But neither yet now are you able."

First Corinthians 2 and 3 show us three kinds of men:

First, there is the soulish man. Such a man merely possesses all the faculties of the soul. We can call him the psychological man. A soulish man is an unregenerated man; he does not have a regenerated spirit and does not have the proper organ to understand God's word. Such a person cannot understand the Bible.

Second, there is the fleshy man. Such a man has God's life and His Spirit within him. But he walks not according to this spirit but according to the flesh. He has a regenerated spirit, but he does not use his spirit or subject himself to the rule of his spirit. He has a spirit, but he does not come under the control of the spirit or allow the spirit to take over everything. The Bible calls this kind of person fleshy. He has a very limited understanding of the Bible. He can only take milk, not solid food. Milk is something that is first digested by the mother. It refers to indirect revelations, revelations that do not come to a person directly. A man who drinks milk cannot receive any direct revelation from God. He receives revelation from other spiritual men, who transfer such revelation to him.

Third, there is the spiritual man. Such a person has the Spirit of God. He operates under the power of the living Spirit and walks according to the principle of the Spirit. The amount of revelation he receives is unlimited. God's Word says that spiritual things can only be discerned by spiritual men.

In order to study the Bible, we have to remember these basic requirements: We must be spiritual and we must walk according to the spirit.

## II. CONSECRATION

### A. The Heart Being Open

The Bible is the word of God. It is full of God's light. Yet this light will only enlighten those who are open to Him. Second Corinthians 3:18 says, "But we all with unveiled face, beholding and reflecting like a mirror the glory of the Lord." The basic qualification for being enlightened by the glory of the Lord is to behold Him with unveiled face. If a man comes to the Lord with a veiled face, the glory will not enlighten him. God's light will only enlighten those who are open to Him. If a man is not open to God, he will not receive God's light. The trouble with some people is that they are closed to the Lord. Their spirit, heart, will, and mind are all closed to God. As a result, the light of the Scriptures will not reach them. Even though the sun is full of light and shines on the whole world, its light will not reach a person who sits inside a room with closed door and windows. The problem is not with the light but with the person. Light will only shine on those who are open to it. This is true of physical light, and this is also true of spiritual light. Whenever we lock ourselves in, light cannot shine through. Some people are closed to the Lord; they can never see God's light. We must not pay attention just to reading and studying; rather, we should ask if we are open before the Lord. If we do not have an unveiled face, the glory of the Lord will not shine on us. If our heart is not open to God, God cannot give us any light.

Light operates according to a law. It shines on those who are open to it, and the amount of shining depends on the amount of openness. This is a law. If all the doors and windows of a room are closed but just one crack is left open, light will still come in. It is not difficult to get the light. As long as one follows this law, he will receive the light. But if he acts contrary to this law, he will not have any light. A man who is closed to God may study and pray much, but he will remain ignorant as far as understanding the Bible is concerned. It is hard for a man to expect any light when he is not open to God. God's light does not come unconditionally. In order to have God's light, one must first fulfill the conditions for receiving it.

Every child of God has a Bible in his hand, but the amount of light each receives from this book is different. Some are completely ignorant of what the Bible says. Others receive some light from reading it. Still others are full of light when they read it. The reason for the difference is that the persons reading it are different. God's light is the same, but the persons are different. People who are open to God can understand the Bible. Others who are closed to God cannot understand the Bible. Some are closed completely, and as a result they are in complete darkness. Others are closed partially, and as a result they receive partial light. Any lack of sight that we experience, whether great or small, complete or partial, means that we are in darkness. We should never consider it a small thing to find ourselves having difficulty understanding the

Bible. If we have difficulty understanding the Bible, it can only mean one thing: We are living in darkness! It is a very serious thing to read God's Word and not understand or receive any light from it.

Next, we should ask what is the meaning of being open to God? Openness comes from unconditional and unreserved consecration. Openness to God is not a temporary attitude; it is a permanent disposition which a man develops before God. It is not an incidental temperament but a continuous practice. Openness to God can only come from unconditional and unreserved consecration. If a man's consecration to God is perfect and absolute, he will have no reservation toward God and will not be closed in any way. Any closedness reflects shortages in one's consecration. Darkness is the result of being closed, and being closed is the result of a lack of consecration. Any time there is a shortage of consecration, there will be reservations. When a man refuses to humble himself before God in any area, he will try to justify himself instead. As a consequence, he cannot understand the scriptural truth related to that same area. As soon as he touches that area, he will try to dodge it. This is the reason we say that darkness comes from being closed, and being closed comes from a lack of consecration. All kinds of darkness come as a result of being closed, and being closed in any area is the result of a lack of consecration and submission.

## B. The Eye Being Single

Many portions of the Bible explicitly speak of light. In Matthew 6:22 the Lord Jesus spoke on the light of the heart, saying, "The lamp of the body is the eye." The Lord did not say that the eye is the light of the body. Rather, He said that the eye is the lamp of the body. Light relates to God, while the lamp relates to us. Light is in God's word, whereas the lamp relates to us. The lamp is the place where light is retained. In other words, the lamp is the place where God deposits His light. It is also the place where we retain and release the light. In order for God's word to shine in us, we must have a lamp within us. This lamp is our eye. "If therefore your eye is single, your whole body will be full of light;

but if your eye is evil, your whole body will be dark" (vv. 22-23). In order for our whole body to be full of light, the Lord specified one condition—our eye must be single.

What does it mean to have a single eye? Although we have two eyes, there is only one focus; they only see one thing at one time. Our eyes are sick if they have two foci and see two objects at one time; neither have a clear view. They are not single. In order for the eyes to see clearly, they must have only one point of focus; they cannot have two foci. In receiving the shining there is the matter of light, and there is also the matter of the seeing of the eyes. If we have never experienced any grace and mercy, we have never experienced any light upon us. But now that we have received grace and mercy, light is upon us. The next problem is not with the light, but with our eye. If our eye is not single, we cannot perceive the light. Many people's eye is not single; they see not just one thing but two things at the same time. Sometimes they see one thing as if it were two things. Light is not clear to them. In fact, they may be in total darkness.

The Lord said, "No one can serve two masters, for either he will hate the one and love the other, or he will hold to one and despise the other. You cannot serve God and mammon" (6:24). Many people do not have light because their eye is not single. The reason their eye is not single is that they are short of consecration before the Lord. What is consecration? It is serving Jehovah alone. A man cannot serve two masters. Either he will hate the one and love the other, or he will hold to one and despise the other; he cannot serve both well. He cannot maintain such a balance. No one can serve the Lord on the one hand and serve mammon on the other hand. All those who try to serve two masters find out sooner or later that they love one and hate the other. We must either consecrate ourselves to the Lord absolutely, or we will serve mammon completely. The Lord said that the eye has to be single. This means that our service and our consecration must be single. Singleness of the eye signifies singleness of consecration.

May the Lord show us this basic principle. If we want to read the Bible, understand its teachings, and receive its revelations, we have to bear one responsibility before the Lord: We have to consecrate ourselves absolutely to Him. Only this will give us light through the Bible. Once we have a problem with our consecration, we have a problem with our seeing. When we have a problem with our seeing, it means that we first have a problem with our consecration. We must be fully convinced that no man can serve two masters.

The other master has a name—mammon. Mammon signifies money and wealth. Much light from the Bible has been veiled because of money. Many people have been veiled from the light of the Bible because of mammon. Many people fail to see the truth in the Bible because they have a problem with money. In addition to God, they have money, and they are not willing to drop their pursuit of money. There is a conflict between the truth and their personal interest. If they could lay aside their personal interest and pursue the truth at all costs, the Bible would be crystal clear to them. Many people sacrifice the teachings of the Bible because they have a problem with mammon. If all the Christians were settled in the matter of mammon, there would be a big increase in the number of obedient ones. We have to heed this warning from God. Whenever we are careless and turn a little to our private interest, God's light will be cut off. In order to see light, we cannot serve mammon. We cannot have two interests. We cannot maintain God's interest as well as our own interest. We can only consider one interest—God's interest. Once our personal interest is taken into consideration, we have two masters, and our eye is no longer single. A double-minded person cannot study the Bible; neither can one who has reservations from private interests. Only those with a single eye can study the Bible.

How can the eye be single? The Lord said, "For where your treasure is, there will your heart be also" (6:21). The amazing thing is that when mammon is under our direction, it will not become a harm but a help to us. When our heart is for mammon, we love money, and it is difficult for our heart to be inclined to God. But if we are able to direct our treasure, we will be able to direct our heart. This is the reason we have to learn to give our treasures away. The Lord said, "For where your treasure is, there will your heart be also." When a man stores up his treasure on the Lord's side, spontaneously his heart will go to the Lord's side. If a man stores up his treasure in heaven, his heart will be in heaven. Where our treasure is, there will our heart be also. If everything we have is with God, our heart will spontaneously be with God, and our eye will be single.

In order to understand the Bible, we need an absolute consecration. Without consecration, our heart will not go to God. One special characteristic of consecration is that it brings our heart to God. When we offer up everything to God, our heart will follow us because our treasure has moved on. There are two kinds of consecration. With one kind, the heart goes first. With the other kind, the heart follows afterward. Some people consecrate their treasure after their heart is touched. Others find their heart following, after they have consecrated their treasure. Whether or not we think our heart will follow us, we only need to take care of our consecration. Whatever we hold on to most dearly should go first. We should give it away in the name of the Lord to needy ones. When our things are given away, our heart goes to the Lord. When all our things are with the Lord, our eye will be single.

Once our eye becomes single, it becomes clear, and light will shine through. The Lord said, "Your whole body will be full of light" (v. 22). What does it mean to have the whole body full of light? It means to have enough light for our feet to walk, for our hands to work, and for our minds to think. In other words, we have light in all areas. Light fills our emotion, will, mind, love, walk, and pathway. We see everything, for our eye is single.

Previously, we have said that only spiritual men can understand the Bible. Now we have to add one more thing: Only consecrated ones can understand the Bible. If a man is not consecrated, he can never read the Bible well. As soon as he opens the Bible, he will come across places that he has held back in consecration, and darkness will be with him. As he reads on, he will come across further unconsecrated areas, and darkness will be with him again. Once darkness is with a man, he cannot hope to receive anything from God. A man must be absolute for God. He cannot serve the Lord on the one hand, and expect to take his own way on the other hand. Some people have argued that they are sincere in seeking God's will, yet they do not know what the Bible teaches. They say they do not know where their problem lies. But this is an excuse; it is not a fact. A man does not know because he does not want to take God's way. If he is truly serious about taking the Lord's way, he will find the way clear and obvious before him. The only kind of person who is never clear is one whose eye is not single.

## C. The Need for Continual Obedience

God grants us revelation of scriptural teachings according to the measure of obedience we render to Him. The more we obey Him, the more light we will receive. If we continue to obey God, we will continue to see. Without consecration, we cannot see. Without a continual obedience, we cannot continue to see. If our consecration is not thorough, the shining will not be great. If our obedience is not fine and detailed enough, the light we receive will not be fine and detailed enough. Therefore, the fundamental issue is consecration. If a man does not understand the meaning of consecration, he cannot understand the Bible. A consecrated person must not only have an initial, fundamental consecration, but he must sustain an obedience before the Lord all the time. Only then will he continually see. The amount of light a man receives depends on the amount of obedience he sustains after his initial consecration. If we are perfect in our obedience, we will be perfect in our seeing.

We should pay special attention to the Lord's word in John 7:17: "If anyone resolves to do His will, he will know concerning the teaching, whether it is of God or whether I speak from Myself." If a man resolves to do God's will, he will know. In other words, obedience is the one condition for knowing. A resolution to do God's will is a condition for knowing God's teaching. If a man has no intention to do God's will, yet wants to know God's teaching, he is asking for the impossible. In order to know God's teaching, a man must first resolve to do His will. This resolution relates to one's attitude. God wants us to be obedient first in our attitude. If a man is obedient to God in his attitude, God's teaching will be clear to him. We should not ask what the Bible teaches. Instead, we should ask if we are willing to obey His word. The problem is with our attitude; it has nothing to do with the teaching of the Bible. Whether or not the Bible will be open to us depends on our attitude towards God. We are responsible for our attitude, while God is responsible for His teaching. If our attitude is right, God will reveal Himself to us and open our eyes immediately. If we supplement this with our obedience, our attitude will be right once again and God will grant us further revelation. First there is a right attitude, and then there is revelation. If we respond to the revelation with obedience, we will have more of the right attitude and will receive more revelation.

Many people claim that they have seen truths in the Bible. Actually, only those who resolve to do God's will have seen them. Only they can claim that their seeing is clear and thorough. The Lord has to do much work in us before we can "resolve" this way. Do not think that light comes without a price. Every seeing is accompanied by a high price; we have to pay a price to see. Sometimes God has to bring a person through two or three experiences before he sees something. Sometimes God has to bring him through six or seven experiences before he sees anything. God's light often comes to us in a reflective way. First it shines on something else, and then it is reflected to us. God's light is often reflective light. We must see light from one angle before we can see light from another angle and then a third angle. Sometimes we need to go through a few experiences before we can see light. If we are disobedient in one thing, we miss the revelation. This is the way God's light acts. Many times we can only see clearly after we have positioned ourselves in different angles. The more price we pay before the Lord, the more light we see. One experience of obedience will lead to another experience and then to even more obedience. One experience of light will lead to another experience and then to even more light. God's will is behind every arrangement He has made.

Whenever a man misses two or three opportunities to obey God, he suffers loss before God.

No matter how much confidence we have in our consecration and obedience, we have to realize that something is wrong with our consecration whenever we are veiled. Whenever we fail to see, our eyes are wrong. God is never short of light, but whenever He sees any unwillingness on our part, He will hold back His speaking. God never forces anyone to do anything, but neither does He release His word in a cheap way. If there is any unwillingness on our part, the Holy Spirit will shy away; He will retreat and not release Himself in a cheap way. If something is wrong with man's consecration, God will not give him any light. It is not a small thing for a man to fail to understand the Bible, because it underscores a problem in his consecration. Spiritual eyesalve involves a price; it does not come freely. Every seeing involves a price. No seeing comes freely.

### III. BEING EXPERIENCED IN PRACTICE

Hebrews 5:14 says, "But solid food is for the full-grown, who because of practice have their faculties exercised for discriminating between both good and evil." The word *practice* can be translated as "habit." There is one condition to receiving God's word—a man must be full-grown. Only a full-grown man can eat solid food. Why must a man be full-grown before he can eat solid food? This has to do with his habit. A full-grown man can take solid food because he is used to it. His faculties are exercised, and he can discriminate between both good and evil. Verse 13 speaks of being experienced in the word of righteousness. To be experienced in the word of righteousness means to be experienced in the word of God. The word *experienced* in Greek has to do with industrial skill; it means to be dexterous. Some workers are unskillful, while others are dexterous. A dexterous worker is one who has passed through much training and who has become skillful in his trade. A person who is experienced in God's word is one who is well trained and skillful in His word. If a man wants to study the Bible and understand God's word, he must be experienced in his practice.

The Bible exposes our condition. The kind of person we are determines the kind of Bible we read. If we want to know what a person is like in character and habit, all we have to do is to show him a chapter of the Scriptures and see what he gets out of it. The kind of person he is will determine the kind of reading he will have. A curious man will find the Bible full of curious things. An intellectual person will find the Bible full of reasonings. A simple-minded person will find the Bible merely a collection of verses. It is a fact that a man's character and habit are often revealed through his reading of the Bible. If a man is not disciplined by God in his character and habits, he will fall into total error, and his reading of the Bible will be spiritually fruitless.

What kind of character and habits must a person have in order for him to read the Bible?

## A. Not Being Subjective

Every reader of the Bible should learn to be objective. No subjective person can understand the Bible. A subjective person is not suitable to be a learner. If we speak to an objective person, he will understand after we speak once. But a subjective person will not understand after we speak three times. Many people do not understand what others are saying, not because they are unintelligent, but because they are too subjective. They live entirely in their mind and cannot take in others' words. They are full of thoughts, opinions, and proposals. Others' words cannot find any ground in them. Their mind may be focused on water, while others may be speaking about mountains. They interpret what they hear and take the mountains to mean mountains with water. A subjective person cannot understand men's word accurately, let alone hear God's word! He cannot understand worldly things, let alone spiritual things.

One interesting thing about those who are good at studying the Bible is that they are all quick to listen. Once others say something, they understand exactly what has been spoken. An objective person can listen to others, and he can also understand the Bible. In contrast, some people do not have any idea what others are saying even after listening once or twice. They have too many things in their head. They are full of thoughts, opinions, and proposals. Others can repeat the same thing to them once or twice, but they will still not get it. In order to find out if we are subjective, we only need to ask ourselves if we understand what others are saying. Can we understand what others are saying even if they speak very briefly? Our days on this earth are limited. If we are subjective, the time that is available to us will be greatly reduced. An objective man can get more from reading the Bible one time than a subjective man can from reading it ten times. A subjective man will miss what he reads even after he reads it once, twice, or even nine or ten times. The Bible will slip by him and not leave any impression in him.

Recall the story of Samuel. When the Lord called him, he went to Eli again and again because he thought Eli was calling him (1 Sam. 3:4-10). God was calling him, but he thought that Eli was calling him. He had heard Eli's voice many times, but this time it was surely not Eli's voice. Could he not tell the difference? Samuel's subjectivity made him think that Eli was calling him. This is the reason he could not differentiate between Eli's voice and God's voice.

The problem with many people is that they will not allow God to break down their subjectivity. No matter how much they study the Bible, they cannot form any impression of it. It seems as if they never hear God's speaking. When we go to the Lord to read His word, our mind must be open to Him. Our opinions, feelings, heart, and everything we are must be open to Him as well. In other words, we cannot be subjective. We must realize the importance of this matter. If a man is not dealt with in this matter, he cannot read the Bible well. An objective person is full of waiting; he waits for God to speak. His inward being waits quietly for God's word. If a man is in this state, he will easily understand what God is saying when he opens to His word. It is unnecessary to ask whether or not a man is spiritual. All we have to ask is what he has received when he reads a certain chapter of the Bible. Some cannot tell us what they have received. This proves that they are subjective. It is not easy for a subjective person to listen to others. He is like those in Hebrews 5:11, who are "dull of hearing." Some people are full of many things, and others' words cannot find any room in them. Subjectivity is a very serious problem. A subjective man cannot hear God's word and cannot touch spiritual things.

## B. Not Being Careless

Second, no one can be careless in reading the Bible. The Bible is a very accurate book. Not a single word of it can be misread or replaced. If a person is somewhat careless, he will miss God's word. A subjective man will miss God's word, and a careless man will also miss God's word. We have to be careful. The more we know God's word, the more careful we will be. A sloppy person has a sloppy reading of the Bible. As soon as we hear a brother speak on the Bible, we know whether he is a sloppy person or a careful person. In reading or memorizing a verse, many people make careless mistakes with crucial words. This is a terrible habit. It is easy for us to become inaccurate in our habit. This leads to an inaccurate understanding of the Bible. In many instances a little carelessness on our part will lead to a misunderstanding of God's word. Let us consider a few examples.

The Bible pays much attention to the distinction between singular and plural forms. We have to differentiate between the singular and the plural form of a word; we cannot be careless about it. Sin and sins are different in the original language. *Sin* in the singular form refers to man's sinful nature, whereas the plural form of the word, *sins,* refers to man's sinful acts. When the Bible speaks of God's forgiveness of man's sins, it uses the plural form—*sins,* as the many sinful acts. God never forgives man's sin—the sinful nature. Sin cannot be forgiven. We need deliverance from our sinful nature (the singular *sin*), but we need forgiveness for our sinful acts (the plural *sins*). The Bible makes a clear distinction between the two.

There is also a difference between sin and the law of sin. If a man is not delivered from the law of sin, he cannot be delivered from sin. Romans 6 is on deliverance from sin, while chapter seven is on the law of sin. If we are a little careless, we will think that these two things are more or less the same.

When we read Romans 6, we may think that the problem of sin is fully settled by the end of the chapter, because at the end of the chapter Paul anticipates the beginning of chapter twelve, where the offering up of one's body and members is spoken of. However, Paul knew clearly that in order to be delivered from sin, we also have to know of the law of sin, and in order to overcome the law of sin, there is the need of the law of the Spirit of life in chapter eight. If we are careless, we may not think that there is much difference between sin and the law of sin, and may thus overlook God's word. God's word is pure; every word has its proper emphasis. If our speaking is careless, we will be led to think that God's word is also careless, and this will frustrate us from understanding His word.

In Romans 7, in addition to the law of sin, there is another law—the law of death. If we are careless, we may think that the law of sin and the law of death are more or less the same. But actually the two are entirely different. Sin refers to one's defilements, while death refers to one's impotence. Willing to do good but not being able to do so is the operation of the law of sin, whereas to will to refrain from evil but not being able to refrain from it is the operation of the law of death. Sin leads one to involuntarily do what he does not want to do, whereas death prohibits one from doing what he wants to do. We are delivered from the law of sin through our death with Christ, and we are delivered from the law of death through our resurrection with Him. Romans 7 shows us not only the law of sin but also the law of death. If we are careless and sloppy, we will miss these truths. It is therefore obvious that only those who are careful and accurate can study the Bible well.

I have heard some say that we put on the righteous robe of the Lord Jesus, that God has given us the righteousness of Christ as our robe of righteousness, and that we are no longer naked, but now can come to God. But the Bible does not teach this. Nowhere in the Bible do we find the righteousness of the Lord Jesus being given to us for our righteousness. The Bible says that God has given us the Lord Jesus as our right-eousness. He has not torn off a piece of the righteousness of

Christ and given it to us for our righteousness. He has given us the Lord Jesus, the very person, to be our righteousness. There is a very big difference here! A careless person will think that the righteousness of the Lord Jesus and the Lord Jesus as righteousness are more or less the same. Little does he realize that the righteousness of the Lord Jesus belongs to Him alone; it can never be transferred to us. Everyone should be righteous before God, and the Lord Jesus also has to be righteous before God. But His righteousness is for Himself. His righteousness is the righteousness He lived while He was on earth. If we can become righteous simply by assuming His righteousness, why did the Lord have to die? The righteousness of the Lord Jesus is not transferable. His righteousness belongs forever to Him alone; no one can share in it. Our righteousness is the person of the Lord Jesus; our righteousness is not His righteousness. In the entire New Testament we only can find the Lord Jesus as our righteousness (except one instance in 2 Peter 1:1, which means something different), never the righteousness of the Lord Jesus as our righteousness. The righteousness of the Lord Jesus qualifies Him to be our Savior. Because He is righteous, He does not need redemption for Himself. The Lord Jesus is fully justified by God. Now God has given Him to us to be our righteousness. The righteousness which God has given us is Christ. We put on Christ. When we have Him on us, we have righteousness. We are not justified by our conduct. We put on Christ, and Christ is our righteousness. We are accepted in the Beloved; we are not accepted in the righteousness of the Beloved. In order to study the Bible well, we have to be accurate and not allow any point to slip by.

Some have said that the blood of the Lord Jesus gives us life. This means that our new life is based on the blood of the Lord Jesus. They say that when we drink the Lord's blood, we acquire His life. They quote Leviticus 17:14, which says that life is in the blood. If we read this verse in a superficial way, we may agree with this teaching. But the blood does not bring us a new life. Blood is for redemption; it is to satisfy God's demand. Exodus 12:13 gives us the governing principle concerning the blood: "When I see the blood, I will pass over you." The blood is for God. It is to satisfy God's demand, not our demand. There is only one instance in the Bible where the blood is spoken of as being for us. In that place it says that the blood is applied to our conscience (Heb. 9:14). However, even the conscience is for God.

What then is the meaning of the word *life* in Leviticus 17? The word *life* there is the same as *soul* in the original language. It refers to the soul-life. The Lord Jesus poured out His soul-life unto death. Isaiah 53:12 says that He poured out His soul unto death. The Lord Jesus shed His blood, that is, poured out His soul unto death for the accomplishment of redemption. He cried on the cross, "Father, into Your hands I commit My spirit" (Luke 23:46). Having said this He expired. His body was hung on the cross, and His soul, through the blood, was poured out for the accomplishment of redemption. (The characteristic of man is his soul. A sinful soul has to die; that is, the seat of a man's personality must die.) At the same time He committed His spirit to God.

John 6 says several times that those who eat the Lord's flesh as well as take His blood will have life. It also says that those who eat His flesh will have life. But at no time does it say that those who only drink His blood will have life. If a man drinks His blood, he also must eat His flesh before he will have life. We have to learn to be careful persons. If we mix up what God has separated, we will end up misunderstanding what He has said. We cannot expound the Bible carelessly. We must study God's word carefully, find the hundreds of instances where the blood is spoken of, and study them one by one before we will see the light. The blood is to satisfy God's demand; it is not to satisfy our demand.

Suppose John Wesley came and told us, "The Lord Jesus' blood will cleanse our heart and eradicate the root of sin from us, and we will sin no longer." What should we say? We should say, "The blood of the Lord Jesus has never cleansed our heart. The Bible never says that the Lord Jesus' blood will cleanse our heart. God has given us a new heart. Man's heart is more wicked than all things and can never be cleansed." The blood is for redemption, not for cleansing. It is for forgiveness, not for sanctification. (There is a difference between sanctification before God and sanctification before men.) Some may ask, "Does not Hebrews 10 tell us that the blood of the Lord cleanses our heart?" [Translator's note: This is the rendering in the Chinese Union Version.] No! The book of Hebrews speaks of the sprinkling of the conscience (10:22). The conscience is only a part of the heart. The only part within man that is conscious of sin is the conscience. The blood satisfies God's demand and also satisfies our conscience's cry. When we realize that the Lord Jesus has redeemed us from sin, spontaneously our conscience will no longer be conscious of sin. The function of the blood in our conscience is not to free us from sin but to remove our consciousness of sin. Freedom from sin is the result of the work of the Holy Spirit. The work of the blood is different from the work of the Holy Spirit; we should never confuse the two.

Before the Lord we have to develop the habit of being accurate. If we are inaccurate, we will sacrifice God's accuracy. If we have a habit of being inaccurate, we will not get anything when we read the Bible. We have to realize how accurate the Bible is. It is so accurate that it has no room for any confusion. We must be trained by the Lord to be accurate.

## C. Not Being Curious

Third, in trying to be accurate, we must not become curious. God's Word is accurate, but we must never search it with a curious mind. If we search God's Word with a curious mind, we will miss the spiritual worth of the book. The Bible is a spiritual book, and we must exercise our spirit before we can understand this book. If the purpose of achieving accuracy is the satisfaction of our curiosity, not the satisfaction of our spiritual needs, we are on the wrong track. It is unfortunate that many people read the Bible with the goal of digging out strange things. Some people have spent a great deal of time trying to ascertain whether or not the tree of the knowledge of good and evil is a vine tree. This kind of study of the Bible is vain. We must remember that the Bible is a spiritual book. We have to touch life, touch the spirit, and touch the Lord. Once we touch the spiritual things, we will spontaneously recognize the literal accuracy of the Word because all spiritual things are intrinsically accurate. But if our premise is not a pursuit of spiritual things, we will be on the wrong track.

Some people like to take the pathway of curiosity. Their study of prophecies is driven by curiosity. They study prophecies not for the sake of waiting for the Lord's return, but because they want to know about the future. There is a big difference between being spiritual and not being spiritual. If we are a curious person, all spiritual and valuable things will become non-spiritual and dead when they fall into our hands. This is a very serious matter. Before the Lord, we have to distinguish between things which are valuable and things which are not so valuable. We have to distinguish between the things which are important and the things which are unimportant. The Lord Jesus said, "One iota or one serif shall by no means pass away from the law" (Matt. 5:18). But He also said that there are "weightier matters of the law" (23:23). The law is so accurate that one iota or serif cannot pass away. But there are also weightier things in the law. Curious ones constantly pick up lighter things and study them. If they keep taking the lighter things, they will end up being lighter persons. As the Lord Jesus said, they are straining out the gnat and swallowing the camel (v. 24). They strain out the tiniest things and swallow the biggest things. This kind of reading is altogether wrong. This error comes from one's disposition for curiosity. If we do not change our disposition, we cannot expect to read the Bible well.

The above mentioned traits—subjectivity, carelessness, and curiosity—are common flaws among men. We must try to overcome these flaws before the Lord. We must be objective, accurate, and non-inquisitive. An objective, accurate, and non-inquisitive character will not come to us in one or two days; we have to discipline ourselves to develop such a habit. As soon as we pick up the Bible, we should read it objectively, accurately, and non-inquisitively. When we have the right character and the right habit, we will know how to read the Bible properly.

# CHAPTER TWO

# ENTERING INTO THREE THINGS
# RELATED TO THE HOLY SPIRIT

In order to study the Bible well, we need to acquaint ourselves with three things related to the Holy Spirit. This is particularly true in reading the New Testament, which has much to do with these three things.

First, the Holy Spirit desires that we enter into His thoughts. In order to understand the words of the Holy Spirit, we must direct our thoughts to the thoughts of the Holy Spirit. This is particularly true in the case of the Epistles. We have to acquaint ourselves with the thoughts of the Holy Spirit before we can understand these writings.

Second, the Holy Spirit has recorded many facts in the Bible. We have to get into these basic facts. If we cannot get into these facts, we cannot understand God's Word. In particular, the Holy Spirit has to open to us the many facts recorded in the four Gospels and Acts.

Third, in our reading, the Holy Spirit will guide us to touch another thing—the spirit. In many instances, it is not enough to know the thoughts; we must get into the spirit behind the thoughts. We must not only know the facts but also must get into the spirit behind the facts. We can find such examples in the Gospels, the book of Acts, as well as the Epistles.

Every Bible reader must get into these three things. Yet only those who have been trained and disciplined can truly know them. We cannot consider them as methods of studying the Bible, for they relate to the very person who reads the Bible. The person must go through some basic training; this is what these issues are all about.

Let us now consider how one can get into these three things.

## I. ENTERING INTO THE THOUGHTS
## OF THE HOLY SPIRIT

In writing the Scriptures, the Holy Spirit had His own purpose and thoughts. A reader of the Bible has to learn not only to read the words and memorize them but also to touch the purpose of the Holy Spirit's writing of the book at the time that He wrote it. The first thing about the study of the Bible is not to busy ourselves with exegesis but to know the intention of the Holy Spirit at the time He wrote the books. We must remember that the value of the words lies not in the words themselves but in the meaning which they convey. The Lord said to the Sadducees, "You err, not knowing the Scriptures" (Matt. 22:29). The Sadducees read God's Word, yet they could not understand it. In reading God's Word, we have to find the reason the Holy Spirit spoke such a word. This leads to another point: Our mind must be well-disciplined.

## A. Merging One's Thoughts
## with the Thoughts of the Holy Spirit

Those who read the Bible must be objective. They must not rely on their own mind. The Holy Spirit has a thought, and our thought has to get into His thought and merge with it. When the Holy Spirit thinks a certain way, we have to think the same way. The two have to flow like two currents in a river, the Holy Spirit being the main current, while we are the subsidiary current. The Holy Spirit is like a big river, while we are like a little stream. The stream has to merge into the river. When the river flows to the east, the stream also flows to the east. The stream may be small, but as long as it flows with the river, it will reach the wide ocean.

Some portions of the Bible focus on facts, others on the spirit, or on thoughts. Those whose focus is on the thoughts are not without spirit and facts. Those whose focus is on the facts are not without spirit and thoughts. Those whose focus is on the spirit are not without facts and thoughts. As we touch the thoughts of the Holy Spirit, we have to be very objective; our whole being should follow the thoughts carried forth by Him. Yet some cannot do this. At the most their thoughts can latch on to the Holy Spirit's thought for ten minutes. They can barely catch up with the Holy Spirit for ten minutes, after which their own thoughts begin to wander off. Such subjective persons can never read the Bible well. The basic requirement for a man to be able to read the Bible is for him to be dealt with in his very person.

It is true that when a man reads the Bible, he needs to exercise his mind. Yet his mind must follow the same direction and flow along the same line as the mind of the Holy Spirit. Wherever the Holy Spirit goes, he should follow. He should find out the Holy Spirit's thought in a sentence, a passage, a chapter, or a book. His entire mind has to be attuned to the Holy Spirit. He has to find out what the Spirit is saying in a passage, what He is thinking, and what His main thoughts and subsidiary thoughts are. The first question we should ask when we read a portion of the Scripture is what is the Spirit's intention in writing this portion. If we do not know the intention of the Holy Spirit behind a portion, we are liable to make a mistake in quoting it at a later time; we may even twist the original meaning of the Holy Spirit. It is not enough for us to merely read the letters or remember the words, memorize the words, or study their meaning in an isolated way. When we read the Bible, we should sense what the Holy Spirit was thinking at the time He was writing it. Putting it in another way, we should sense the thoughts of Paul, Peter, John, and the others when the Holy Spirit spoke through them. Our thoughts must merge with the Spirit's thoughts before we can understand the Bible.

A story was told of a believer who took a journey through the forty-two stations that the Israelites passed through from Egypt to Palestine. Where the Israelites turned, he turned. Where they detoured, he detoured. He went through the entire journey this way. Later he wrote a book recounting the journey. He did not choose his path; he took Moses' path. This is the way we should read our Bible. We must not determine the direction ourselves; we have to go where the Spirit is going. Paul went down to Jerusalem, and we should go down with him to Jerusalem. He felt a certain way and thought a certain way, and we should feel and think the same way. We should not have our own independent direction. We must follow the direction of the writers of the Bible. In other words, we must follow the direction of the Spirit. The thoughts of the writers of the Scripture should be the thoughts of the readers of the Scripture today. The writers of the Bible were inspired by the Holy Spirit to think a certain way. The readers of the Bible should also be inspired by the Holy Spirit to think the same way. If our thoughts can closely follow the thoughts the Spirit bore at the time of the writing of the Scriptures, we will understand what the Bible is saying.

## B. Finding the "Trunk" and the "Branches"

Some parts of the Bible are subject texts, while others are explanatory words; some are primary in importance, while others are ancillary in function. Some are like the trunk of a tree, while others are like the branches of the tree. We should not follow the branches and lose sight of the trunk. Of course, we should not pay attention just to the trunk and forget about the branches. We should find out what the Holy Spirit is saying in a passage, how He is saying it, how many things are spoken of, and how many words He has used to achieve His goal. Our mind should follow these things step by step. We have to catch up with the mind of the Holy Spirit. The Spirit has a subject to His speaking, and He also has words explaining the subject. When we are halfway through our speaking, we may digress from the subject with a word of explanation. These are "branches." Branches do not grow all the way to the top of the sky. Likewise, the Spirit can digress from His subject with a word of explanation for five or ten verses, but He always comes back to the "trunk." We must not dwell on the explanations all the time; we must follow the Holy Spirit and turn back to the subject. Many of the Epistles are structured in such a way that explanatory words are interwoven into subject passages. We must differ-entiate between the "trunk" and the "branches" before we can understand what we are reading. We cannot rush through in our reading. When the Holy Spirit makes a detour, we have to make the same detour. When the Holy Spirit turns back to the subject, we also have to turn back to the subject. We have to be very tender and very careful to not put any trust in ourselves or have any assurance in our flesh. This is the way to catch up with the thoughts of the Holy Spirit.

There are "trunks" and "branches" in the words of the Bible. Yet these "trunks" and "branches" are linked together to form one unified whole. For example, in writing the book of Romans, Paul's intention was not only to give us 3:23, 6:23, or 8:1. The whole book conveys one unified thought; it is one complete entity. There is no fragmentation whatsoever. We must not take a few verses out of context and just expound them. It is all right for us to borrow a verse, but we have to differentiate clearly between borrowing a verse and making an exegesis of the verse. Even when we borrow the verse for some other use, we have to understand the context of the verse. Otherwise, we fall into the error of taking things out of context.

If our mind is trained, it will be strong enough to *sustain the light*. Light comes in a flash, and it has to be captured and sustained. If our mind is not trained to join itself to the mind of the Holy Spirit, we will not have enough thoughts to capture and sustain the light when it comes to us in the form of a revelation. This is the reason our mind has to be trained; it has to be altogether objective and responsive to the leading of the Holy Spirit. The Holy Spirit has His own way of expression. For example, Romans 1 and 2 speak of man's sin. Chapter three speaks of redemption, chapter four of faith, chapter five of the sinner, chapter six of the death of the sinner, chapter seven of two laws, and chapter eight of the Holy Spirit. Chapters nine to eleven give some examples. Chapter twelve speaks of the Christian and the church, and finally, chapters thirteen to sixteen speak of the walk and conduct of a saved person. In reading this book, we have to understand the intention of the Holy Spirit at the time He spoke these words. In every section the Spirit had some main thoughts. First, He spoke about man's sin and then about the solution of sin and the accomplishment of God's righteousness. Then He went on to speak of faith and of the obstacle to faith—human work. But there is more to man's problem than his sin; there is the problem of his person. Therefore, in chapter six the Spirit spoke of the crucifixion of the sinner (the old man). The solution to man's sin lies in his faith in the Lord's death *for* him, whereas the solution to the man himself lies in his faith in his death *with* the Lord. In chapters nine through eleven, the nation of Israel is used as an illustration of God's grace and faith. Chapter twelve then covers the condition of a consecrated Christian. From chapter one through chapter sixteen, we can identify the "trunks" clearly. Paul was very clear in expressing his feelings through these points. There are also the "branches"; we find some of them even in the very first section. In covering the subject of man's sin, the Holy Spirit digresses to speak of the Gentiles and then the Jews, and then He turns back to the main thought. In reading the Bible, we have to follow the thought of the Holy Spirit closely.

## C. Two Kinds of Training

There are two ways to train our mind. First, we can separate the subject text from the explanatory words. It is not a bad idea to go through the New Testament and put parentheses around passages that the Spirit provides as words of explanation. The words inside the parentheses are the "branches," while the words outside the parentheses are the "trunks." If we skip the verses in the parentheses and read the rest, we will get an idea of the main subjects of the various portions.

Let us try this out with the book of Romans. Romans 1:1 says, "Paul, a slave of Christ Jesus, a called apostle, separated unto the gospel of God." This clearly is the introduction to the book of Romans. Verses 2-4 say, "Which He promised beforehand through His prophets in the holy Scriptures, concerning His Son, who came out of the seed of David according to the flesh, who was designated the Son of God in power according to the Spirit of holiness out of the resurrection of the dead, Jesus Christ our Lord." This is an explanation of the gospel. Therefore, these three verses are "branches" which can be put inside a parenthesis. Verse 5 says, "Through whom we have received grace and apostleship unto the obedience of faith among all the Gentiles on behalf of His name." This again is the subject text. If we go on this way with the rest of the book of Romans, we can single out the verses which are subject text. We can underline the subject text with one color pen and the explanatory words with another color pen. In the first pass, we do not have to read the explanatory words. Read the subject text first, and then the explanatory words later. First, find the main thoughts of the Holy Spirit, and then insert the explanatory portions little by little. What is this gospel? It is something which was "promised beforehand through His prophets in the holy Scriptures." God first promised the gospel and then sent the Lord Jesus to accomplish this gospel. In His accomplishment, there are two parts. First, there is the part according to the flesh. Second, there is the part according to the Spirit. The first part deals with His life on earth as the son of Mary. The second part deals with His life in heaven as the Son of God. The four Gospels cover the part of Him according to the flesh, while the Epistles cover the part of Him according to the Spirit. In reading this portion, we can jump directly from verse 1 to verse 5 and leave verses 2 through 4 for later. Always take care of the subject text first, and then the explanatory words later. In this way we can get into the thought of the apostle at the time he wrote the book. We should read the whole Bible this way. In particular, we should read the Epistles this way. Every servant of God should know the text portions of a book as well as the explanatory portions. This is the first step.

What benefit do we derive from taking this first step? It enables us to know how much of the teaching in a portion relates to the subject and how much relates to explanations. In serving as a minister of the word, our speaking has to have main subjects and explanations. Although our functioning as ministers of the word is not as perfect and profound as that of the first apostles, it is the same in principle. Once we distinguish the subject text from the explanations, we will realize to our surprise that the Bible always provides sufficient explanations, both in quantity as well as in degree.

We will worship the Lord for the absolute perfectness of the Word. We will also find that as soon as we are just slightly excessive in our use of explanations and illustrations, our whole message will become weak. We have to pay attention to the way the Bible explains things. We should never over-explain. We should only provide explanations for the parts that others do not understand. Explanation is for the purpose of helping others to understand, but we should not be excessive in our use of it. Some speakers are short in explanation, which loses the listeners. Others are too long in explanation, which drags down the message. We should observe the perfect balance in the Word. We should always learn to separate the subject text from its explanations. In order to do this, we have to be objective. Once we become subjective, we certainly will fail.

Second, we have to try to paraphrase the text portion with our own words. We have to rewrite the text portions of the Bible with words that we can understand. For example, Romans 1:1, 5, and 6 are text verses. The wording in these verses belongs to Paul. After we understand what Paul has said, we should try to express the same thing with our own words. At the beginning we should only work with the text portions; we should not work on the explanatory words within the parentheses. This kind of exercise is like our experience as students: The teachers told us a story, and we wrote it down in our own words. We must know what the story is about before we can write it down. This kind of paraphrasing requires that we be objective, that we understand the meaning of the Bible, and that we do not add our own thoughts to it. We have to train ourselves to be a follower of the thoughts of the Holy Spirit. We have to fashion our thoughts according to the thoughts of the Holy Spirit.

Of course, we can make mistakes in our paraphrasing. The only thing we can do when we make mistakes is to correct them the next time. If we still make mistakes, we should correct them again. The more we correct ourselves, the more accurate we will become. Once a person learns this lesson, it will be easy for him to understand God's Word. The most important thing is to put ourselves aside. Once we become proud or subjective we are finished. We have to learn to be objective, meek, and humble. A meek and humble mind will find it easy to follow the mind of the Spirit. Every reader of the Bible has to learn this lesson.

## II. ENTERING INTO THE FACTS RECORDED BY THE HOLY SPIRIT

### A. The Impression from the Facts

When reading the Bible, the Holy Spirit next requires that we capture an impression from the facts. The Bible is not all teachings. A great part of it is facts, history, and stories. The Holy Spirit desires that the facts, history, and stories produce a certain impression within us. Once we have an impression of these facts from the Holy Spirit, it will be easy for Him to convey God's word to us. If these facts do not produce an impression in us, God's word will not take hold in us and will not produce the proper effect in us.

The impression that we are speaking of here does not refer to a general familiarity with the stories. It refers to a view concerning certain characteristic points that make a lasting impression in our mind. In the Bible every incident has its characteristics. Without understanding these characteristics, we cannot understand God's word. In reading a contract, it is not enough to check whether or not there is a signature on it; we must check whose signature is on it. The impression that we are speaking of here is not a general impression but an impression of its special character. Once we discover the special character, we can learn what God wants to say through them. It is possible that a person can remember and even relate a biblical incident to others but not be able to point out its special character. This means that he does not understand God's word. The New Testament contains the four Gospels, the Acts, the Epistles, and Revelation. For the Epistles, we have to get into the thought of the Holy Spirit. For the four Gospels and Acts, however, our heart has to be open to God's Spirit, and we have to allow Him to impress us with the facts. We have to realize the difference between these facts and other facts, and we have to sense the special characteristics that lie behind these facts.

An impression works like a photograph. The film in a camera is a slide of glass or a thin piece of plastic coated with a chemical—silver bromide. Decades ago, one square inch of film could only hold tens of thousands of silver bromide particles. This is the reason the photographs produced at that time were not very sharp; they were granular in appearance. Later, film improved, and the granular look disappeared. The image is now much clearer because each square inch of film holds millions of silver bromide particles. In the same way, the finer our inner constitution is, the more impression we will retain. The coarser we are, the less impression we will retain. If our heart and spirit are open to God, and if our feelings are refined, the flashing of the facts of the Holy Spirit before us will generate a strong impression within us. If we are fine and tender, we will see two things. First, we will locate the emphasis in God's Word and the focus of His revelation. Second, we will know what God wants to say behind the facts, and we will be able to tell the difference between these facts and other facts.

A coarse person will never see the fine points in the Bible. A man must be tender, and his feelings must be very sensitive before God's word can stamp a clear image within him. He will not only catch a glimpse of the general contour, but he will have an accurate impression of the fine points and lines. He will be clear about every delicate and intricate point behind the facts.

## B. Tender Feelings

Many people seek to know the fine and tender aspects of the Bible. Yet without fine and tender feelings, they cannot grasp these tender points. Consider the four Gospels and Acts. All five books are records of Jesus. More facts are revealed about the Lord Jesus through these five books than through all the Epistles. We need to have fine and tender impressions of these facts related to the Lord Jesus. Let us consider some examples.

## 1. *Examples of Contrasts*

### a. *Zaccheus and the Two Disciples on the Way to Emmaus*

In contrasting Luke 19 with Luke 24, we find a marked difference between the Lord's stay at Zaccheus's house and His entering the house with the two disciples who were on the way to Emmaus. The Lord volunteered to enter Zaccheus's house. But in the case of the two disciples, it seems as if He wanted to go on. A fine person will detect two completely different attitudes of the Lord here. With Zaccheus the Lord took up a despicable sinner. He was not an ordinary tax collector; he was a chief tax collector. The Lord did not wait for his invitation; He volunteered to go into his house. Zaccheus no doubt wanted to see the Lord. But he was conscious of his small stature and his bad reputation, and he was too ashamed to invite the Lord. Under these circumstances, the Lord said, "Zaccheus, hurry and come down, for today I must stay in your house" (19:5). Here was a seeking sinner who dared not ask the Lord to stay with him. The Lord invited Himself to his house. He understood Zaccheus. His feelings were tender. If our feelings are tender enough, we will understand the Lord.

The two disciples on the way to Emmaus were backslidden. Their eyes were veiled, and they did not recognize the Lord. The Lord walked with them, spoke to them, and expounded the Scriptures to them. When they were drawing near to the village, He acted as though He would go farther (24:28). The Lord's attitude toward the two disciples was different from His attitude toward Zaccheus. Zaccheus faced great obstacles; he was haunted by unspoken embarrassments. The Lord was gentle to him and volunteered to go to his house. The two disciples on the way to Emmaus knew the Lord already. But they had become backslidden. Although they heard so much from the Lord, they were still heading for Emmaus. This is the reason the Lord acted as though He wanted to go on. He stayed only after they implored Him. In one case, there was a man coming towards the Lord. In the other case, there were two men walking away from the Lord. Accordingly, the Lord's attitude was different. We have to touch the tender feelings of the Lord Jesus before we can realize who Jesus of Nazareth is and who this One is whom God intends to reveal to us.

### b. The Two Occasions of Peter's Fishing

In Luke 5 Peter had fished throughout the night and caught nothing. Yet the Lord Jesus told him, "Put out into the deep and let down your nets for a catch" (v. 4). The fishermen let down the nets and caught a great number of fish. Before this they caught nothing. Now, surprisingly, they enclosed a great number of fish. Peter fell down at Jesus' knees, saying, "Depart from me, for I am a sinful man, Lord" (v. 8). In John 21 we find Peter and other disciples fishing again. The Lord asked them, "Little children, you do not have any fish to eat, do you?" They answered Him, "No." And He said to them, "Cast the net on the right side of the boat" (vv. 5-6). Then they caught many fish. The fishing in Luke 5 revealed the glory of the Lord Jesus to Peter. When this great glory broke upon him, he saw that he was a sinner who was unworthy of the Lord's presence. In the fishing expedition after the Lord's resurrection, Peter jumped into the sea and swam ashore when he recognized the Lord (John 21:7). He had no more interest in fishing when he recognized the Lord. In both cases he had the same revelation. But in the first case, the revelation caused the man to know himself and to beg the Lord to depart from him, having previously known nothing of himself. In the second case, the revelation drew this man who already knew the Lord to a more intimate relationship with Him. Once we identify the differences between these two cases, we have a proper impression of the facts. In all these matters, we need a solid impression of the facts.

### c. The Lord's Feeding of the Five Thousand and Mary's Anointing of Him

Two incidents are recorded in all four Gospels: the Lord's feeding of the five thousand with bread, and the anointing of the Lord by Mary. After the Lord fed the five thousand, He ordered the disciples to gather the broken pieces that nothing would be lost (John 6:12). This is quite amazing. The

Lord performed a miracle to feed men with bread, yet He asked the disciples to gather the broken pieces lest they be wasted. Later a woman came, broke the alabaster flask, and anointed the Lord's head with ointment. Some disciples said, "Why has this waste of the ointment been made?" But the Lord Jesus said, "She has done a noble deed on Me" (Mark 14:3-7). Here we see two contrasting things: the feeding of the bread and the anointing of the Lord. In one case, nothing was wasted. In the other case, everything seemed to be wasted. Nothing produced from a miracle was to be wasted, yet something worth over three hundred denarii could be poured on the Lord and not spared. The ointment was worth three hundred denarii; it was not spent to feed five thousand but to be consumed by the Lord in an instant. It was not a gathering up but a breaking apart. It was not twelve baskets but one alabaster flask. All these are contrasts. In the case of God's Son performing a miracle, even the leftovers are to be gathered up. But He does not consider it too much to receive the consecration of something equivalent to three hundred denarii. All four Gospels record this story, and everywhere that men preach the gospel, they are to remember this story. Consecration should go as far as the gospel goes. Wherever the gospel goes, an absolute offering of consecration to the Lord has to follow. The reaches of the gospel must be the reaches of man's consecration and ointment. We must have a solid impression of this fact.

### d. The Judgment of the Lord and the Judgment of Paul

Sometimes it is meaningful to compare the four Gospels with Acts. We can compare the judgment the Lord faced with the judgment that Paul faced. When Paul was judged, he said that he was a Pharisee and a son of Pharisees (Acts 23:6). This was different from the case of the Lord Jesus. We treasure our brother Paul. But the best son that the world can produce is merely a son of man. Jesus of Nazareth, however, is the only begotten Son of God! When we compare the two, we find that one is God's only begotten Son, while the other is merely a child of God. One is the Master, while the other is the servant. One is the Teacher, while the other is the student. Although Paul's attainment was high, he cannot be compared to his Lord. We have to be fine and tender. Only then will we come to know the Lord depicted in the Gospels and the apostles depicted in the Acts. If we are not tender, we will not be impressed with anything. Even if the Lord wants to show us something, we will not be able to prostrate before Him and worship Him. A careless man treats the Bible as if it were just ordinary stories. He glosses over everything, and it is difficult for the Holy Spirit to impress him with anything.

### e. The Lord's "Passing Through" and Paul's Being "Let Down"

Once the Lord Jesus was reading the Scriptures in the synagogue in Nazareth. After He finished, He spoke a little, but the crowd took Him to the brow of a hill so that they might throw Him down the cliff. Yet He, passing through their midst, went away (Luke 4:29-30). How solemn and dignified He was! He was not like Paul, who had to be let down through the wall and lowered in a basket (Acts 9:25). We are not saying that Paul was wrong in any sense. We are saying that there is a difference in nature. The Lord passed through the crowd and went away. These few words, "passing through their midst, went away" (Luke 4:30), should give us some kind of impression. When the Lord passed through those who wanted to kill Him, the crowd could only watch; they could do nothing. How dignified and noble is our Lord!

## 2. Examples of Similarities

### a. Dissatisfactions with the Lord

Many impressions in the Bible have to be studied by the way of contrast. This is the case with the five examples mentioned above. Other examples show similarities, and one has to put them together to form an integrated picture.

#### 1) The Lord Falling Asleep in the Boat

Matthew 8:23-27 speaks of the instance when the Lord Jesus crossed the sea with the disciples. Suddenly a great tempest rose up in the sea. The Lord was asleep, and the disciples were afraid. In Matthew's record the disciples said, "Lord, save us; we are perishing!" (v. 25). But Mark 4:38 has something more to say: "Teacher, does it not matter to You...?" That means that they questioned how He could sleep so soundly. The Lord Jesus rebuked the wind and the waves, and they were stilled; then He turned and rebuked the disciples for their little faith. (Notice the order of events according to Mark and Luke. Before the Lord rebuked the disciples, He rebuked the wind and the waves.) The Lord had a basis for rebuking the disciples because He had said that He would cross to the other side. Since He had said it, it must be so. There was no need to worry even if there were winds, waves, or whatever along the way. The Lord Jesus was teaching them the lesson of faith. What were they putting their faith in? They should have trusted in the Lord's word: "Let us go over to the other side" (Mark 4:35). With the Lord having said that they would go over to the other side, it was not possible for them to end up at the bottom of the sea. Yet the disciples did not have faith in this. This is the reason the Lord rebuked them.

It is interesting that we never find the Lord apologizing to anyone. Under normal circumstances, the more lessons a man learns before the Lord, the more he has to apologize to others. The more disciplined a person is, the more he discovers others' dissatisfaction with him, and the more frequently he will need to apologize to them. The Lord Jesus is unique in that He never had to apologize to anyone. It seems as if the disciples thought that they were right and the Lord was wrong. The winds and the waves were fierce, and the disciples were perishing. Did this not matter to the Teacher? But the Lord did not wake up to apologize. The absence of an apology is an expression of His glory. He knew that He did not oversleep, and He knew that He was not wrong. When He said to cross to the other side, He meant that they would cross to the other side. There was not one wasted word in Him, and no one can make Him apologize for anything. This shows the glory of our Lord!

### 2) The Touch of the Woman
### with the Flow of Blood

In Mark 5 we have the story of the woman with the flow of blood who came to touch the Lord Jesus. Here we find the same principle. When the woman touched the Lord, He turned around and asked who had touched Him. The disciples said, "You see the crowd pressing upon You and You say, Who touched Me?" (v. 31). This was said in somewhat a rebuking tone. The Lord did not say, "I am sorry; I asked the wrong question." Instead, He turned around to see who was touching Him. He was, in effect, saying, "Someone is touching Me, but you do not know it. Your eyes are on the pressing ones, but My eyes are on the touching one." Outwardly speaking, the Lord appeared to be wrong; it seemed as if the disciples were justified in their indignation. But in reality the mistake was with the disciples, not with the Lord. The Lord never apologized once to anyone. This is most glorious, and our heart cannot help but worship Him.

### 3) The Death of Lazarus

In John 11 we find another instance of men being dissatisfied with the Lord. Martha said to the Lord, "Lord, if You had been here, my brother would not have died" (v. 21). She was blaming the Lord for arriving late. She was saying in her heart, "I sent men to ask for You a long time ago. Why did You not come sooner? Because of Your delay, my brother has died and has been buried." The phrase *if You had been here* expresses Martha's extreme unhappiness. Apparently, Martha's words were absolutely right. But the Lord did everything with deliberation. He purposely stayed where He was for two more days (v. 6). In man's eyes this was a delay, but the Lord Jesus purposely delayed His coming. Our Lord never apologizes to anyone, because He is never wrong. We apologize, because we are often wrong. If we refuse to apologize, it means that we are arrogant. The more humble and meek we are, the more we will apologize. Although our Lord is humble and meek, He never apologizes, because He is never wrong. When we are unhappy with Him, our unhappiness does not make Him feel guilty, for He knows what He is doing.

We can find many cases like these in the New Testament. In reading the Bible we have to learn to apply the principle of gathering together all the portions which speak of similar things. From the above three examples, we can discover one glorious fact: The Lord never takes back one word that He has said; He never turns back on a pathway that He has trodden. What a glory this is! Was it more glorious for Lazarus to be healed or for him to be resurrected? The Lord knew that it was more glorious for Lazarus to be resurrected. If we believe, we will see God's glory.

### b. Attempting to Teach the Lord

#### 1) "This Ointment Could Have Been ...Given to the Poor"

Sometimes men were not only dissatisfied with the Lord; they even tried to teach the Lord. The disciples said, "Why has this waste of the ointment been made? For this ointment could have been sold for over three hundred denarii and given to the poor" (Mark 14:4-5). They were teaching the Lord. The disciples could think of another way to dispose of the ointment—sell it and give it to the poor. But the Lord knew what Mary was doing. He said that she was doing a noble deed. The Lord never does one thing or says one thing that He is not clear about. He needs no one to correct Him. Only a foolish man will try to correct the Lord or teach Him.

#### 2) "God Be Merciful to You!"

When the Lord indicated to the disciples that He had to go to Jerusalem, Peter said, "God be merciful to You, Lord!" What did the Lord say? He said, "Get behind Me, Satan!" (Matt. 16:21-23). Peter wanted to teach the Lord, but it did not work. On the contrary, he only exposed his own foolishness.

#### 3) "What Sort of Woman This Is"

Once the Lord Jesus ate at the house of Simon the Pharisee. A woman stood at the Lord's feet weeping, wetting His feet with her tears, and wiping them with the hair of her head. Simon thought in his heart, "This man, if He were a prophet, would know who and what sort of woman this is who is touching Him" (Luke 7:39). Here we should pay attention to Simon's spirit. He seemed to be saying, "Look what kind of woman she is. How can You allow her to come near to You at Your feet?" Although Simon did not open his mouth, the Lord knew what he was thinking, and He spoke about different kinds of forgiving. In effect the Lord was saying, "You, Simon, did not wash My feet, because you have experienced little forgiveness. This woman experienced much forgiveness. This is the reason she wet My feet with her tears." Once we have such an impression, we will realize how foolish it is for man to try to be the Lord's counselor! At the same time, we will know a Jesus of Nazareth that we did not know before.

### c. The Lord Likes to See Men
### Asking Great Things from Him

In studying the Gospels carefully, we find that the Lord took pleasure in men asking Him for great favor. The greater men's requests were, the happier the Lord was to answer them.

#### 1) "If You Are Willing, You Can Cleanse Me"

Consider the story of the leper in Mark 1. According to Jewish regulations, a leper could not come in contact with any man. Any person who came in contact with a leper was defiled by uncleanness (Lev. 13—14). Here a leper came to see the Lord Jesus. The very act of coming to the Lord was quite presumptuous. We should have a strong impression of this fact. As soon as a leper appeared on the scene, we probably would react. Unless a man was ready to sacrifice himself and give his all, he would jump back at the sight of a leper and say, "You are hurting me! I cannot touch you. Why do you come to me?" When the leper came to the Lord, he did not ask whether the Lord could cleanse him. Instead he said, "If You are willing, You can cleanse me" (Mark 1:40). This was a very piercing statement. He put all the burden on the Lord! It was all a matter of whether or not the Lord was willing.

This was not an ordinary prayer. It was something that put the Lord's heart to the test. The Lord simply could have said, "Be clean," and the leper would have been cleansed. But the Lord did not merely utter a word; He identified Himself with the leper's situation. He touched the leper with His hand and said, "I am willing; be cleansed!" (v. 41). If he was not cleansed, the Lord would become defiled. What a risk this would have involved! We must have the proper impression of the story before we can understand the actual picture. The Lord was ready to put Himself into the leper's situation. He joined His holiness and purity to the leper. Either both would be clean or both would be defiled. Either both had to go outside the camp or both could return to the camp. The Lord was ready to spend, and what a spending that was!

### 2) "They Removed the Roof"

Mark 2 records four men carrying a paralytic to the Lord Jesus. Being unable to bring him to the Lord because of the crowd, they removed the roof where He was, and lowered the paralytic to the Lord (vv. 3-4). We should have an impression of this picture. Many people were surrounding the Lord. He was quite busy. But now another group lowered a paralytic from the roof! We should realize that the Lord was not just busy; He was also speaking in a borrowed place. When the roof was removed, it had to be patched later. What trouble this was! But the Lord did not say, "Do not do this again." Instead He was happy that someone would come to Him with such a big demand. It seems that the bigger the demand was, the happier He felt. This shows us what kind of Lord He is. If we do not have a clear impression of what the Lord has done, how can we say that we know Him?

### 3) "Jesus, Son of David, Have Mercy on Me!"

As the Lord was traveling, Bartimaeus cried out, "Jesus, Son of David, have mercy on me!" (Mark 10:47). Many people rebuked him and tried to silence him. But he cried out much more. The Lord Jesus was not particularly fond of noise and excitement. Matthew 12:19 says, "He will not strive nor cry out, nor will anyone hear His voice in the streets." This was what the Lord Jesus was like. But here was a man crying out in a loud way. He wanted the Lord to have mercy on him, and the Lord healed him. The Lord is happy to see men asking great things from Him. He wants men to open their mouths wide. He is happy to give grace in abounding measure.

### 4) "Even the Little Dogs Eat of the Crumbs Which Fall from Their Masters' Table"

The story of the Canaanite woman gives us a clear picture of this principle. The bread was for the children. Yet she said, "Yes, Lord, for even the little dogs eat of the crumbs which fall from their masters' table" (Matt. 15:27). This was a request that she had no right to ask. But the Lord likes to see men asking Him in this way. He not only granted the request and healed her daughter, but He praised her for her great faith. We can find many examples like these in the Gospels. If we form the proper impressions of these things, we will know the Lord's heart through them.

### 5) "I Believe; Help My Unbelief!"

After the Lord came down from the Mount of Transfiguration, a father brought his demon-possessed son to Him. The Lord first rebuked the man (Mark 9:14-29). He did not rebuke the leper who came to Him, and He did not rebuke the paralytic whose friends removed the roof. They were all presumptuous, yet the Lord Jesus was happy with what they did. But here the father first brought his sick son to the disciples. When they could not heal him, he brought him to the Lord. The Lord asked the father, "How long has this been happening to him?" He answered, "From childhood. And it has often thrown him both into fire and into water to destroy him. But *if You can do anything,* have compassion on us and help us." He came to the Lord for healing, but he was not sure if the Lord could heal. He said, "If You can do anything." The Lord picked up his words and said, "If You can." Following this, He said, "All things are possible to him who believes." The Lord seemed to be saying, "Why are you asking if I can? You should realize that all things are possible to him who believes! It is not a matter of whether or not I can, but of whether you believe." We have to visualize the situation at that moment. The man came halfheartedly. He intended to come to the Lord, but he did not have the faith. He did not fully trust in the Lord's healing. In pleading for His mercy, he qualified his prayer with the words, "If You can." The Lord rebuked this word severely. He is not pleased when men ask Him for less. He is not afraid when men say to Him, "You have to do it whether or not You are willing." But the father did not say this. In effect he was saying, "If You can do it, do it. If You cannot do it, so be it. Your disciples could not do it. I will not press for anything if You cannot do it either." The Lord rebuked him, saying, "You say, If You can. All things are possible to him who believes" (v. 23). When the Lord said this, the father, "crying out...said, I believe; help my unbelief!" (v. 24). As soon as he was rebuked and his mistake was exposed, he turned and believed. He put all the responsibility on the Lord. This is a beautiful picture! The higher a man's demand is, the more the Lord is pleased with it. The less a man asks for, the less the Lord is pleased. We have to be a tender person and allow the Lord to impress these things upon us. Once we see them, we will realize that all the Gospels are filled with the Lord's glory.

### d. Isolated Examples

#### 1) "Who Is My Neighbor?"

In the story of the good Samaritan in Luke 10, we should focus on the Lord's word. The lawyer asked, "Who is my neighbor?" (v. 29). The Lord's answer was based on something completely different. Verse 27 says, "You shall love...your neighbor as yourself." The word *yourself* refers to the lawyer, and the *neighbor* must be someone other than the lawyer. In effect the Lord was saying, "If you, the lawyer, can love your neighbor as you love yourself, you will have eternal life." Verse 29 says, "But he, wanting to justify himself, said to Jesus, And who is my neighbor?" He thought that the Lord Jesus was asking him to love others, and he wanted to find out who these others were. The Lord responded with the story of the good Samaritan, and at the end, asked,

"Which of these three, does it seem to you, has become a neighbor to him who fell into the hands of the robbers?" The lawyer answered, "The one who showed mercy to him." Jesus said, "Go, and you do likewise" (vv. 36-37). The lawyer asked who his neighbor was, and the Lord Jesus responded by asking who was the neighbor of the man who fell into the hands of the robbers. In other words, the lawyer was the one who had fallen into the hands of the robbers. The One who showed mercy to him was his neighbor. The neighbor does not refer to any man; it refers to the Savior. The Lord showed the lawyer that the neighbor is the Lord Himself. He said, "Go, and you do likewise." This means that the lawyer should do his best to love that Samaritan. Many people have turned the parable around. They think that the Lord wants them to be the Samaritan. They do not realize that they cannot go to the cross to forgive sins, and they cannot be lifted up to bring down the Holy Spirit. Only He has the wine and the oil. Only He has the beast, the inn, and the denarii. We are not the Samaritan. It would be totally wrong to ask the man who fell into the hands of the robbers to be the Samaritan. The neighbor whom the Lord referred to was the Samaritan. This means that the Lord came to be our Neighbor; He came to save us, to provide us with the beast, the wine, which signifies the forgiveness, the oil, which signifies the life, the inn, which signifies the church, and the denarii, which signify the gifts and grace. These things He gives until He returns. When the Lord tells us to love the Samaritan, He is telling us to love Him. We have to learn to touch the fine points in this passage. This is the way to read the stories in the Bible.

### 2) The Lord's Dignity and Glory

When men sought to catch the Lord in the garden of Gethsemane, He stepped forward and said to them, "Whom do you seek? They answered Him, Jesus the Nazarene. He said to them, I am....They drew back and fell to the ground" (John 18:4-6). The Lord simply spoke one sentence, and they drew back and fell to the ground. What a glory we find here!

Our Lord prayed at the garden of Gethsemane, but He did not plead for anything at the court, before the high priest, or before the magistrate. This One is far above all. He is the Lord, yet He was judged. Who was actually judging whom? The high priest was the one who was agitated. He was the one who stumbled in words. Our Lord remained calm. When He appeared before the magistrate, it was the latter who became nervous; he was the one who was aimless in his questions. The Lord did not bother even to answer the questions. Jesus of Nazareth is God. Although He was put on trial, He did not lose His dignity or His honor.

In the garden of Gethsemane, He told the disciples to be watchful with Him (Matt. 26:38), but He did not ask them to supplicate for Him. Paul needed the brothers in Rome to pray for him (Rom. 15:30), but the Lord did not need anyone to pray for Him. He is the Son of God, and He does not need anyone to supplicate for Him. He asked the disciples to pray because He did not want them to enter into temptation (Matt. 26:41); He was asking them to pray for themselves. Here we can observe once again the Lord's dignity and honor.

He lived in poverty on earth, yet He did not ask anyone for any money. He prayed to God in the garden, yet He pleaded with no one in the court. Who is like the Son of God? The throne is glorious, but the glory of the judgment and the cross is even greater. We have to worship Him and say, "You are Lord! You are God!"

### 3) The Lord's Hiding of Himself

The Lord always hid Himself; He did not like to have a name for Himself. After He healed the leper, He charged him not to tell anyone (Matt. 8:4). After He drove out the company of demons, He charged the previously possessed man to go home and to speak what *God* had done for him (Luke 8:39). After He opened the eyes of two blind men, He charged them not to let anyone know about it (Matt. 9:30). After God revealed Him to Peter as the Christ, the Lord charged the disciples not to tell others (16:20). On the Mount of Transfiguration, He was the only One who shone in glory. Yet when they came down from the mount, He charged the disciples not to tell others what they had seen (17:9). We find a similar case in John 7. The Lord's own brothers did not recognize Him. They told Him, "Depart from here and go into Judea... for no one does anything in secret and himself seeks to be known openly. If You do these things, manifest Yourself to the world" (vv. 3-4). His brothers said this because even they did not believe in Him. Yet He said, "My time has not yet come" (v. 6). After His brothers went up, He also went up to the feast, not to perform any miracles there, but to teach. Here we touch our Lord's glory. Everyone who tries to draw attention to himself is eager to present his work before men. But the Lord never wanted to purposely expose Himself before men. The Gospels are full of such records. He stood before men only when there was the absolute necessity for it. He did not like to tell others who He was. Even after He had performed a miracle on the blind man, He did not tell him who He was immediately. He held back the revelation of who He was until He brought the man into some further enlightenment (John 9). Before this, He would not tell him who He was. We need to know our Lord!

## C. Impressions Resulting from Lessons

In order to understand the history both in the Old and the New Testament, we have to have the right impressions. In order to have the proper impressions, we have to be a tender person. This is the reason we have to go through proper lessons before the Lord. If a person has a low discernment, he cannot be expected to appreciate the dignity of the Lord Jesus when he reads the Gospels. If he is dealt with even a little, he will know what dignity is, and when he comes to the Bible again, he will have more appreciation of the dignity of the Lord Jesus. If he does not know the meaning of dignity and glory, how can he be expected to form an impression of the Lord's dignity and glory? We have to receive the proper lessons from the Lord. His nature has to be added into us daily. In this way, our feeling towards God's Word will be finer and finer every day. We will have deeper and deeper impressions every day, and we will understand more and more of His Word every day. We should remember the principle that whoever has, it shall be given to him, and he will abound; but whoever does not have, even that which he has shall be taken away from him (Matt. 13:12). We should never neglect our lessons. Otherwise, we will lose what we have.

### III. ENTERING INTO THE SPIRIT OF THE SCRIPTURES

In order to study the Bible well, we have to acquaint ourselves with the thoughts of the Holy Spirit as well as the facts from the Holy Spirit. In addition, we have to enter into the spirit of the Scriptures.

## A. Touching the Spirit behind the Word

God's Spirit prompted men to write the Scriptures, and whether it is history or doctrines, each portion has a spirit of its own. Every portion of the Bible has its own unique spirit behind the word. The Holy Spirit expresses Himself through the spirit of man. When we say that the Holy Spirit rejoices, the Holy Spirit is not just rejoicing within Himself; rather, the Holy Spirit is rejoicing through man's spirit. In the same way, when we say that the Holy Spirit grieves, the Holy Spirit is not grieving within Himself; rather, the Holy Spirit is grieving through man's spirit. Hence, when the Holy Spirit enters man's spirit, the condition of the Holy Spirit becomes the condition of man's spirit. Putting it another way, we can say that the condition of man's spirit is the condition of the Holy Spirit. When the Spirit of God recorded history, He recorded the facts of history. However, this history contained not only facts, it also captured a certain spirit. We can say that certain feelings and conditions of the Spirit are impregnated within each portion of the Word. In the same principle, in the writing of the Epistles, the Holy Spirit did not just convey doctrines and thoughts. Behind every passage there is the feeling of the Spirit. The Bible is not merely a book full of facts and doctrines. On the surface there are the words. Underneath the words there are thoughts, and behind the thoughts is the spirit. If we only touch the words, our reading of the Bible is too superficial. If we can form a proper impression and enter into the thoughts behind the words, we have gone deeper. However, if we remain in this realm, our understanding is still very limited. Behind every word of God is a certain spirit. The feeling of the Holy Spirit and the condition of the writers govern these writings. When we study the Bible, we have to touch the spirit behind the word.

There is an inseparable link between the word and the spirit. The ministry of the word is the release of the spirit. Anyone who stands up to be a minister of the word has to release his spirit. If he cannot release his spirit, he cannot be a minister of the word. Moreover, the spirit must be right. One must have a right spirit before he can have a right ministry of the word. We often fail as ministers of the word because the spirit cannot match the word that is released. There is nothing wrong with the words that are spoken, yet something is wrong with the spirit. The words are strong, but the spirit is weak. However, the ministers of the word in the Bible did not have this problem. Their spirit matched the content of their writings. Behind every passage and every book, there is a proper spirit; this spirit is impregnated in the word. In releasing the ministry of the word, we need the word on the surface and the spirit to back up the word. In receiving the ministry of the word, we also have to touch the spirit behind the word. When we study the Bible, our purpose is to receive the ministry of the word. As such ones, we have to touch the spirit behind the word. If we do not touch that spirit, our understanding of the Bible will be very shallow indeed. At most we will have some doctrines and facts; we will not find spiritual nourishment. If God's word is only impressions and thoughts to us, it cannot become our food. God's word must become spirit before it can become our food. Our food can only come as we touch the spirit behind the word. The essence of the Bible is spirit. If we do not touch the spirit behind a passage, we have not touched that portion of the Scriptures yet. In reading the Bible, we have to touch the spirit, that is, the particular spirit behind a portion of the Word.

### B. How to Touch the Spirit behind the Word

How can we touch the spirit behind the word? We must point out that this can be realized only through the discipline of the Holy Spirit, not by man's effort. The discipline of the Holy Spirit means that God's Spirit comes in to replace man's work. God's Spirit arranges everything in the environment and operates until our spirit matches the spirit of the Scriptures. Even though the two spirits cannot be identical, they can be similar in character. Only then will we touch the spirit behind the Word. Only when the two spirits are similar can we touch that which lies behind the Word. If they are not similar, we cannot touch anything. We reach the highest peak in the study of the Scriptures when our spirit harmonizes with the spirit of the writers of the Bible. When our spirit matches the spirit of the writers, we touch the spiritual content of the Word.

The spirit that lies behind the Word is a very particular spirit. In other words, it is very definite; it is not hidden behind the Word in a hazy way. The Holy Spirit first molded the writers of the Bible; He sealed His approvedness on them. Then He used them to write the Scriptures. Their spirits were perfected, and through their spirits the Holy Spirit operated to write the words that became the Bible. In other words, the inspiration of the Holy Spirit included not only the supply of words to men but also the preparation of these men to be proper vessels. Because these vessels were filled with the Spirit, they were able to write the words they wrote. Hence, the spirit behind the Bible is perfect, dynamic, unerring, and accurate. The Holy Spirit worked on the writer's spirit and put His mark of approval and satisfaction on it. He concluded that these men would not restrict Him or limit His freedom; He could freely express His views. Even His slightest breath was not inhibited by such men. We can say that the Bible is the Holy Spirit's very breathing. It conveys men's spirit, but when it is released, it also conveys the very breath of the Holy Spirit. The Holy Spirit has absolute freedom in these men. Their spirit has become almost indistinguishable from the Holy Spirit, and its manifestation is almost the same as the manifestation of the Holy Spirit. The writers of the Bible were led by the Holy Spirit in this way in their writing of the Holy Scripture. When we read the Bible, our spirit must also be led by the Holy Spirit to match the spirit of those who were prompted to write the Bible. This is the only way we can touch the spirit behind God's Word. The study of the Bible is not merely a study of the words of the Bible. Neither is it merely an understanding of the meaning of the Bible. The Lord has to guide us to the point that our spirit becomes one with the spirit behind the Word.

The Bible is recorded in written words, not in audible sounds. Except some psalms which use the word *selah,* there is no other indication in the whole Bible as to whether we should read it loudly or softly. Yet when we read it, we should know something from the writing. If we cannot distinguish between the "loud" portions and the "soft" portions, how can we distinguish the condition of the spirit?

Many portions of the Word are words of pleading and beseeching. They are like the pleadings and implorings of a gospel preacher when he invites men to believe in the Lord. The preacher pleads because he is aware of the sufferings of the sinners and sees the danger of their ways before the Lord. He pleads because he is full of the Lord's compassion, and he wants the sinners to turn. He knows that a passage of the Scripture is a word of pleading because he senses the compassion, sympathy, and understanding for the sinners behind the words. If he reads this passage without the feelings that are behind it, it will be hard for him to understand it.

Some words of the Bible are words of rebuke. If a man has never been broken by the Lord, he will not know what these words mean when he reads them. He will not know the meaning of rebuking under the pressure of the spirit; he will only know to rebuke when he is angry. He will not realize that the spirit within the words may be different even though the words of rebuke are the same.

We must learn to touch the spirit of the Bible with our spirit. In order to train our spirit, the Holy Spirit arranges all kinds of environments for us. We should realize that the best and most important training in our life comes from the discipline of the Holy Spirit. This discipline rests in the hand of the Holy Spirit; it does not rest in our hand. He dispenses this discipline gradually. As we are disciplined continually, our spirit is tempered to a proper condition. Our spirit is adjusted on the left and on the right; it receives a little smiting here, a little joy there, and a little patience and a little stripping elsewhere. As a consequence, our spirit is tempered to fit exactly the passage we are reading. When our spirit is tempered to a proper condition, the words will be transparent and clear to us, even though the thoughts governing the words have not changed at all. When we speak about them, what comes out may be the same words, and the thoughts behind the words may still be the same, yet we will begin to know and be clear about the things we are speaking of. This is not a result of clarity in thoughts or words but of clarity in the spirit. This is something deeper than words and thoughts. It is so deep that the only thing we can say is that we are clear, that everything has become transparent to us. This is what happens when God's Spirit matches our spirit with the spirit of His Word.

Touching the spirit of the Bible is not a matter of methods. It is a matter of whether or not a person has been dealt with by the Lord. If our spirit has not been brought into harmony with the spirit of the writers of the Bible, at most we can be a teacher; we cannot be a prophet. At most we can touch the doctrines; we cannot touch the spirit. If our very person has not been dealt with and disciplined by God, and if God has not operated in us systematically, we will be shrouded with a veil when we come to the Word. No matter how hard we try, we will be separated from it by a great distance. Our spirit must be dealt with. We must allow God to deal with us severely. During the first few years of our Christian life, we may understand some doctrines and facts, but touching the spirit is something more difficult. If our spirit is not ready, it cannot be put to use. We need a certain amount of time, at least a few years, for the Lord to adjust our spirit, to temper it, and to break it. Once the spirit is broken, it will be easy for the Holy Spirit to bring us into harmony with the condition of the Scriptures. Actuality, it takes many years for our spirit to match the spirit of the Bible. Man's wisdom is useless in this matter. It may help us to understand the word sooner, but it will not help us to touch the spirit behind the Word. No matter how productive our imagination is or how powerful our perception is, we cannot get into the spirit of the Word. Only the Holy Spirit can bring our spirit into harmony with the spirit of the Bible. Only then can we get into the spirit of a particular portion of the Word.

## C. Moving from Sameness in Quality to Increase in Capacity

The Holy Spirit is matching our spirit with the spirit of the Bible. This refers to a match in quality, not to a match in capacity. The spirit of the Lord Jesus is thousands of times greater than our spirit. He is the only begotten Son of God! Sameness in quality means that we have a little share in the spirit that He possesses. They are the same in kind, but they are not the same in degree. However, the discipline of the Holy Spirit can carry us further, from just a qualitative matching of our spirit with the spirit of the Bible to an actual increase in the capacity in our spirit. The Lord increases the capacity of our spirit with His Spirit. This involves a process that goes on continuously like feeding. Today the Lord dispenses something to us. Tomorrow He will dispense more things to us. As the dispensing increases, the capacity of our spirit increases. As we begin to understand the Bible, we begin the process of feeding, and as we are fed, our capacity increases. *The starting point in our understanding of the Bible is a matching in the quality of the spirits, while the consummate issue of our understanding of the Bible is an increase in the capacity of our spirit.*

Suppose a man has a terrible temper. He cannot read God's Word no matter how hard he tries. After God disciplines him, he will have a little patience. This patience is not the result of a conscious effort on his part, nor is it a kind of manmade endurance; it is the spontaneous result of the work of the Holy Spirit. After he acquires this kind of spirit, his reading of God's Word will result in the ministration of Christ. God's word will supply his spirit and enrich it. He will receive more and more, and his capacity will increase little by little. The discipline of the Holy Spirit first brings a man's spirit into harmony with the spirit of the Bible as far as the quality is concerned. Then there can be an increase in capacity as well. This increase in capacity comes from the discipline of the Holy Spirit through the environment, as well as through the words of the Bible. The Holy Spirit does the breaking work through His discipline in the environment. At the same time, through the words of the Scripture, He brings us the supply so that our capacity will increase. The more the Holy Spirit ministers His word to us, the richer we become. Every ministration of the Holy Spirit brings more riches to us. Through the continual ministration of the Holy Spirit through the word, our capacity is continually expanded.

If we are continually fed by the word, the Bible will be continually fresh to us. In the eyes of man, the Bible was completed eighteen or nineteen hundred years ago, and it bears no more significance to us than just a recapitulation of the thoughts and concepts presented at the time of its writing. In reality, however, the Spirit that was present at the time of the writing of the Scriptures is still with us today. When we read the Bible today, we should read it as if it was written today. Whenever we read the Bible with our spirit, it is a new book to us. Although historically this book was completed over eighteen or nineteen hundred years ago, it is not old in any way, because it is a book written in spirit. We become tired of many books after reading them a few times. But we are not tired of the Bible even after reading it dozens of times. This is because it is a book in the spirit. If we touch the Bible according to the letters or according to our thoughts, it will become old to us before very long. But if we read it by the spirit, it is new to us every time. Whenever we find a portion of the Word tasteless, it is not the portion itself that is tasteless but our spirit that has failed to function. Every portion of the Bible is full of the spirit. If our spirit is strong enough, every passage will be precious to us. But if we do not read the Bible with our spirit, even a book as precious as Romans or a passage as wonderful as the sermon on the mount will be tasteless and meaningless to us. Actually, it is not the Bible that has become meaningless, but our spirit which has become fallen. Once our spirit becomes fallen, the Bible becomes tasteless to us. When our spirit is not strong, we lose the taste for reading. But when our spirit is strong, the Bible will be a fresh book, as one that has just been completed.

The spirit of the Word is indeed rich. A man should not presume that his spirit is strong and that he can meet all the demands. Only those who have passed through the dealings will know a little about the Bible. The amount of dealing one experiences dictates the amount of his understanding. Because we have only experienced limited dealing, we remain at the place where we were before, being ignorant of many things. It is imperative that we pass through the discipline of the Holy Spirit. The more discipline we go through, the more we learn. At a certain point, when our spirit somewhat matches the spirit of God's word, we will see light. Revelation will come, and we will be fed.

## D. The Spirit Being Fine

Why do we treasure a portion of the Scriptures so much, yet another brother sees nothing precious about it? This is because we capture the spirit of that portion of the Scripture, while the other brother does not. I am not saying that the other brother does not have a spirit. I am saying that his spirit is not in step with the spirit of this portion of the Word. Sometimes, he may treasure another portion of the Word, yet we have no feeling about it. We are as closed to that portion as he is to our portion of the Word. Our spirit must be fine, and we must be sensitive to many things. Once our spirit is fine, we will be sensitive to our many different circumstances. The finer our spirit is, the wider the scope of our knowledge of the Word will be. The scope of our knowledge of the Bible depends on the amount of discipline we have received from the Holy Spirit. Our feelings can only become rich and fine after passing through much discipline. As the discipline increases, the feelings increase. A man understands a certain portion of the Word only after he has passed through a certain kind of discipline. Hence, it is important that we gain rich experience by going through dealings. If we are not rich in such experiences, our feelings will not be rich, and if our spiritual feelings are not rich, our knowledge of the Bible will not be rich.

## E. Two Examples

Let us consider two examples in the Bible and from them find the meaning of entering into the spirit of the Word.

### 1. The Story of Jacob

Jacob was a clever, cunning, and selfish man. In everything he considered himself first, never others. He was very conniving, and he resorted to all kinds of schemes to achieve his goal. This was the reason God had to deal with him. When he was born he held to his brother's ankle and fought with him. But Esau became his father's love, while he was set aside. Jacob tried everything he could to usurp his brother's blessing. But in the end what he got was not blessing but wanderings. He served Laban, who changed his wages ten times. He wanted to marry Rachel but had to take Leah first. On his way back to his father's land, Rachel died, while Leah survived. His heart was with a few of his sons, being particularly fond of Joseph. Yet Joseph was sold by his brothers, who dipped his garment in blood and deceived Jacob. He thought that Joseph was devoured by the beasts, and said, "I will go down into the grave unto my son mourning" (Gen. 37:35). Then he shifted all of his hopes to his youngest son, Benjamin; yet Benjamin was taken into Egypt. Day by day Jacob suffered God's dealings. His days were hard. Proverbs 13:15 says, "The way of the treacherous is hard." Jacob's days were full of sufferings as a result of his stubbornness and craftiness.

We should not think that Jacob's experience at Peniel was a cheap one (Gen. 32:22-32). He insisted that God bless him. It seems as if he was saying, "My father had to bless me. Everyone had to bless me. God must also bless me!" He was a cunning man. In everything he wanted to gain something. He wanted God's blessing, and God promised that he would be called Israel. Yet his blessing did not come immediately; it came decades later. At Peniel God touched the hollow of his thigh, and he was crippled. From that day forward God's work took a turn in him. Yet the next day we see the same old Jacob on his way to meet his brother Esau. He split up his children into groups, thinking that he would preserve the second if the first suffered calamities. He put his beloved Joseph and Rachel in the last group. He was still exercising his own wisdom. He was still scheming.

Although Jacob was cunning, he became a very spiritual man in his old age. When he went down to Egypt in his advanced years, he was very much different from what he was before. "And Joseph brought in Jacob his father, and set him before Pharaoh: and Jacob blessed Pharaoh" (Gen. 47:7). This is a beautiful picture. Pharaoh was the ruler of a nation, yet as he stood before Jacob, Jacob appeared taller than he! This man had gone through years of wrestling and was finally at rest. When he stood up, Pharaoh, the monarch of an empire, stooped down! If the old Jacob had been there, he probably would have acted the same as he did when he met Laban, setting his eyes on Laban's possessions. Pharaoh's possessions were many times more valuable than Laban's. But Jacob was a stricken man. His eyes were no longer on these things, but on the lessons he had learned from God. Spontaneously, he stood tall before Pharaoh. "And Pharaoh said unto Jacob, How old art thou? And Jacob said unto Pharaoh, The days of the years of my pilgrimage are a hundred and thirty years: few and evil have the days of the years of my life been, and have not attained unto the days of the years of the life of my fathers in the days of their pilgrimage" (vv. 8-9). Here we find the release of this man's spirit. He said, "Few and evil have the days of the years of my life been." This described his whole life. This old man had gone through many sufferings before he could say this word. Our spirit has to enter into his spirit. A man who has experienced God's smiting work is never haughty. We have to remember God's promise to Abraham: "And I will make thy seed as the dust of the earth" (13:16). God also promised Isaac, saying, "And I will make thy seed to multiply as the stars of heaven" (26:4). At the time of Abraham, there was only a single descendant; there was no household, much less a nation. By the time of Jacob, there were seventy people in his household. God's promise was realized in his household. Yet Jacob did not boast of this. On the contrary he said, I "have not attained unto the days of the years of the life of my fathers in the days of their pilgrimage." He was able to say this because he was smitten and humbled. "And Jacob blessed Pharaoh, and went out from before Pharaoh" (47:10). He came in blessing Pharaoh, and he went out blessing Pharaoh. He had something to give to others. What a beautiful picture! The aged Jacob had changed. Now he was Israel; he was no longer the same. Here we should touch his spirit.

"And Jacob lived in the land of Egypt seventeen years: so the whole age of Jacob was a hundred forty and seven years. And the time drew nigh that Israel must die" (47:28-29). We should notice that at his birth he was called Jacob but at his death he was called Israel. "And he called his son Joseph, and said unto him, If now I have found grace in thy sight, put, I pray thee, thy hand under my thigh, and deal kindly and truly with me; bury me not, I pray thee, in Egypt: but I will lie with my fathers, and thou shalt carry me out of Egypt, and bury me in their buryingplace. And he said, I will do as thou hast said. And he said, Swear unto me. And he sware unto him. And Israel bowed himself upon the bed's head" (vv. 29-31). What a beautiful picture this is! We have to touch the spirit here. Here was a man who by nature was cunning and hard, who would do everything to satisfy himself and would ask for nothing less than the best. Yet on that day he said to his own son, "If now I have found grace in thy sight." What tenderness! "I pray thee...deal kindly and truly with me." He asked for kindness and truthfulness. "Bury me not, I pray thee, in Egypt." God's place for him was Canaan. His promise could not be fulfilled in Egypt. Under God's sovereignty he was about to die. Yet he asked for kindness and truthfulness that he would be buried in God's promised land. Jacob was not doubting God's promise. On the contrary, he asked Joseph to swear because he believed in God. He wanted Joseph to see the solemnity of the matter. Unless we touch his spirit, we will not understand what he was doing. "And Israel bowed himself upon the bed's head." What a wonderful scene!

Let us also read Genesis 48. Verses 2 through 4 say, "And one told Jacob, and said, Behold, thy son Joseph cometh unto thee: and Israel strengthened himself, and sat upon the bed. And Jacob said unto Joseph, God Almighty appeared unto me at Luz in the land of Canaan, and blessed me, and said unto me, Behold, I will make thee fruitful, and multiply thee, and I will make of thee a multitude of people; and will give this land to thy seed after thee for an everlasting possession." He remembered God's promises to him. He knew clearly that it was God's blessing that gave him seventy people in his household. God had promised that he would be fruitful and multiply and that the land of Canaan would be given to his seed.

Verse 5 says, "And now thy two sons, Ephraim and Manasseh, which were born unto thee in the land of Egypt before I came unto thee into Egypt, are mine; as Reuben and Simeon, they shall be mine." He placed Joseph's two sons under God's promise. "As Reuben and Simeon, they shall be mine." He accepted Joseph's two sons as his own sons. At his old age, Jacob was clear about everything.

Verse 7 says, "And as for me, when I came from Padan, Rachel died by me in the land of Canaan in the way." This incident touched him deeply. He still remembered it at his deathbed. How tender, mature, and sweet is a man who has passed through God's chastisement! How rich was his deposit! The conniving Jacob had been changed; he became an entirely different man.

Verses 8 through 10 say, "And Israel beheld Joseph's sons, and said, Who are these? And Joseph said unto his father, They are my sons, whom God hath given me in this place. And he said, Bring them, I pray thee, unto me, and I will bless them. Now the eyes of Israel were dim for age, so that he could not see. And he brought them near unto him; and he kissed them, and embraced them." When Isaac was old, his eyes were poor, and he was deceived. When Jacob was old, his eyes were also poor, but his inward eyes were very clear. Unlike Isaac in his old age, who was greedy for venison, Jacob was ready to bless. "And he brought them near unto him; and he kissed them, and embraced them." Here we sense the overflow of compassion of an old man.

Verse 11 says, "And Israel said unto Joseph, I had not thought to see thy face: and, lo, God hath showed me also thy seed." Here we find again a spirit stricken by God.

Verses 12 through 14 say, "And Joseph brought them out from between his knees, and he bowed himself with his face to the earth. And Joseph took them both, Ephraim in his right hand toward Israel's left hand, and Manasseh in his left hand toward Israel's right hand, and brought them near unto him. And Israel stretched out his right hand, and laid it upon Ephraim's head, who was the younger, and his left hand upon Manasseh's head, guiding his hands wittingly; for Manasseh was the firstborn."

Verses 17 through 19 say, "And when Joseph saw that his father laid his right hand upon the head of Ephraim, it displeased him....And Joseph said unto his father, Not so, my father: for this is the firstborn; put thy right hand upon his head. And his father refused, and said, I know it, my son, I know it." Although Jacob's eyes were dim, his inward being was not dim. He knew what God wanted him to do. "He also shall become a people, and he also shall be great: but truly his younger brother shall be greater than he, and his seed shall become a multitude of nations." We should remember that Isaac was muddled in his blessing but Jacob was very clear in his blessing.

Verse 21 says, "And Israel said unto Joseph, Behold, I die; but God shall be with you, and bring you again unto the land of your fathers." This is faith. How real a living faith is! At that time all their future seemed to lie in Egypt. No household had more prospect than they had in the land of Egypt. Yet Jacob said, "God shall be with you, and bring you again unto the land of your fathers. Moreover I have given to thee one portion above thy brethren, which I took out of the hand of the Amorite with my sword and with my bow." In whose hand was this land at that time? It was not in his hands. Yet he said, "I have given to thee one portion." In effect he was saying that even though Joseph was governor over Egypt, his land was not Egypt, but Canaan. "Moreover I have given to thee one portion above thy brethren." He knew that Ephraim and Manasseh were two persons, and therefore that Joseph should have a double portion.

Genesis 49 gives us one of the greatest prophecies in the Bible. Jacob foretold what would happen to every one of his sons and every one of the tribes. He blessed by faith and in obedience, and everything was clear to him.

Verses 29 through 30 say, "And he charged them, and said unto them, I am to be gathered unto my people: bury me with my fathers in the cave that is in the field of Ephron the Hittite, in the cave that is in the field of Machpelah, which is before Mamre, in the land of Canaan, which Abraham bought with the field of Ephron the Hittite for a possession of a buryingplace."

Verse 33 says, "And when Jacob had made an end of commanding his sons, he gathered up his feet into the bed, and yielded up the ghost, and was gathered unto his people." At his birth he was busy holding on to the heel of his brother. At his death he gathered up his feet properly into the bed. He was not hasty or restless and was not struggling with God in any way.

We must observe that the Bible is full of spirit. When we contact this spirit with our spirit, we touch the tender and precious points of the Bible. We have to contact not only the stories and the doctrines in the Word. We have to touch the spirit behind the Bible with our spirit.

### 2. Paul Revealed through 2 Corinthians

Among Paul's Epistles, 2 Corinthians stands out as the book that reveals more of his spirit than any other book. Other Epistles tell us the revelations that Paul received, but this Epistle reveals to us the very person Paul was. Other Epistles speak of his ministry, while this Epistle speaks of his person. It shows us the riches, purity, and meekness that lay within his spirit. He was more misunderstood by the Corinthians than by any others. The Corinthians were uninhibited in saying all kinds of things about Paul. Yet what clarity and purity we find in the spirit of Paul's word to them. We can say that Paul's spirit was more released through the Corinthians' misunderstanding than through his trials which he faced in the last chapters of Acts. If we read through 2 Corinthians sentence by sentence, we will understand not only Paul's thoughts but also his spirit. We will notice that even when he was rebuking, his spirit was not provoked. Only those who are full of love can rebuke others. If our spirit cannot match Paul's spirit in 2 Corinthians, we may take his boasting to the Corinthians as a kind of complaint. But we should realize that while the words may be the same, the spirit can be totally different. Two persons can say the same thing and mean the same thing; they can even use the same terms. But their spirits can be very different.

We have listed only two examples. Throughout the Bible we can detect such a spirit. Some places are more obvious, while others are less obvious. Either we should give up reading the Bible altogether, or we have to bring our spirit up to the level of the spirit of the Bible. Moses went through many trials. If we have not entered into the spirit of these trials, we will not understand these portions. The book of Psalms is much deeper than the book of Jeremiah. If our spirit does not match the spirit of the psalms, we cannot understand them. The same holds true for the New Testament. If our spirit does not match the spirit in the books of the New Testament, we cannot understand them. Therefore, we have to learn some basic lessons before the Lord. We must be a spiritual person before we can read the Bible. We must be consecrated, and we must not be subjective, careless, or curious. We must have impressions of the facts, and we must enter into the thoughts of the Holy Spirit. After we have all of these, we still need more. Our spirit has to be up to the standard, and we have to be dealt with by the Lord to the point that we can identify with the spirit behind every portion of the Word. We must have this kind of spirit before we can understand God's Word. If we do not touch the spirit, we will only have letters. We may even misunderstand God's Word or turn the meaning all around. When a father speaks to his children, his children must touch the spirit of their father's words. If they do not and then spread his words around, they may end up saying something entirely different. There is a spirit behind all the words of the Bible. If we neglect this spirit, we will not understand the feeling and the motive behind the words, and we will run the risk of missing the content of the speaking altogether. Let me repeat: If a man has not been dealt with by the Lord, it will be hard for him to read the Bible. We have to remember that the way to study the Word is to have our being dealt with by God.

# SECTION TWO

# METHODS OF STUDYING THE BIBLE

# INTRODUCTION

In the previous section we took note of the person who studies the Bible. Let us now turn our attention to the method of studying the Bible. In studying the Bible, we must not only be right persons, but we must also have the right methods. We will consider the subject of method under three categories. First, we will consider the keys to studying the Bible; second, we will consider the practice; and third, we will consider the plan.

# CHAPTER THREE

# KEYS TO STUDYING THE BIBLE

## I. BY SEARCHING

John 5:39 says, "You search the Scriptures." Acts 17:11 says, "Now these people were more noble than those in Thessalonica...examining the Scriptures daily..." The first thing in studying of the Bible is to examine it. The word *examine* means "to search" in the original language. In other words, if we want to find out anything from the Bible, we have to search for it in the Scriptures themselves. We have to look for it like rummaging through our closets for a lost article of clothing. We examine many things for the purpose of searching for one thing. Among the many words that God has spoken, there is one word which we need at the present moment. There is one word which will render us spiritual help at this particular time for this particular occasion. We may have received a revelation, and we need a word to explain and express it. Or we may need to find the Scriptures' revelation concerning a certain subject. In order to find these things, we have to search through God's Word. We should approach the Bible with a searching mind. To search means to read with deliberation and to devote time and care to our reading. We have to study every word until we understand it. While we are reading we have to ask, "When was this written? Who wrote it? Who was it written to? Under what circumstance was this written? What was the feeling behind this word? Why was it written? What was the purpose for writing it?" We should ask these questions one by one slowly, look for the answers carefully, and not stop until we have found what we are looking for.

Sometimes in answering a question, we have to search through the entire Old and New Testaments for things related to the subject. We have to examine the entire Bible carefully word by word, lest we miss something important through oversight. Sometimes we know what we are looking for in God's Word. At other times we do not even know what we are looking for. Sometimes we only need one thing, but sometimes we need many things. In our search we have to exercise the utmost care and meticulousness. We cannot allow one word or phrase to slip past us. We must bear in mind that the Bible is God-breathed (2 Tim. 3:16). This means that every word and phrase is God's word and is full of life. We have to devote the utmost attention to our reading.

Patience is needed in reading the Bible. If we do not understand something, we should come back to it a second time. We should read until we understand what it says. If God enlightens us and opens our eyes the first time, we can thank the Lord for it. But if He does not enlighten us or open our eyes the first time, we should go back and study it carefully the second, third, and even hundredth time. If we come across anything in the Bible that we do not understand, we should not be anxious. There is no need to force ourselves to mentally apprehend or understand it, and there is no need to insist on receiving light from it. Things that come from the head will not produce an "amen" from the spirit. Doctrines that are formulated by the mind are rejected by the spirit. We must not study God's Word according to the mind. Rather, we should be patient, and search slowly. When God's time comes, He will show us something.

A great mistake that many people make is that they do not search the Scriptures themselves. Rather, they read what others have said. No matter how much help others can render us, we have to read and search the Scriptures ourselves. We must not seek help from others all the time while neglecting to read the Bible ourselves. On the one hand, we do not despise prophecy; we need the edification of the prophets as well as those of other ministries. Yet at the same time we have to study the Bible ourselves. We cannot simply receive help from others while neglecting to read it ourselves.

## II. BY MEMORIZING

Paul told the Colossians, "Let the word of Christ dwell in you richly in all wisdom" (Col. 3:16). In order to have the word of Christ dwelling in us richly, at least we have to memorize the Scriptures. Of course, memorization alone may not result in God's word dwelling in us. But we can say that if one does not memorize God's Word, he certainly cannot have it dwelling in him richly. If a man merely memorizes the Scriptures with his mind, but his heart is not receptive or open to God and he is not submissive or meek, his memorization will not result in God's word dwelling in his heart. Yet if a man thinks that there is no need to memorize God's word because he only needs to be meek and submissive and open and receptive to God, he also will not be able to have God's word dwelling in his heart.

Paul told the Ephesians, "Remember the words of the Lord Jesus, that He Himself said, It is more blessed to give than to receive" (Acts 20:35). In order to remember the Lord's word, we have to memorize it. If we do not memorize it, we cannot remember it. The Lord Jesus memorized the Scriptures while He was on earth. He was able to quote the words of Deuteronomy to deal with Satan's temptations (Matt. 4:1-10). When He entered the synagogue in Nazareth, He was able to open up to the book of Isaiah and speak forth the commandment and commission He had received from God (Luke 4:16-21). This shows that our Lord was very familiar with the Scriptures. For this reason we should give all the more diligence to study and memorize the Word. If we do not memorize it, we will forget what we have read, and we will reap little benefit from it. The young people in particular should try to memorize and recite it as they read it with a searching mind. We should spend time during the first few years of our Christian life memorizing the Scriptures. Many portions of the Word need to be memorized. For example, Psalm 23, Psalm 91, Matthew 5—7, John 15, Luke 15, 1 Corinthians 13, Romans 2—3, and Revelation 2—3 all need to be memorized. Those with a strong memory can memorize over ten verses a day. Those with a poor memory can memorize at least one verse a day.

All we need to do is spend five to ten minutes a day to study a verse thoroughly and to search and memorize it. In about six months we will finish a book like Galatians or Ephesians. A book like Philippians can be finished within four months, and a book like Hebrews can be finished within ten months. The Gospels may take a longer time. But even a book like the Gospel of John can be memorized in eighteen months. If the young brothers and sisters would study the Bible diligently from the beginning of their Christian life and memorize at least one verse a day, they would be able to recite most of the important verses in the New Testament in four years. The above discussion pertains to those with a poor memory. Those with a better memory can do better. But even those with a poor memory can memorize one verse a day during the first four years of their Christian life. If they would do this, they would build up a solid foundation for themselves in their understanding of the New Testament.

If our hearts are open to God and meek in attitude, it will be easy for us to memorize the Scriptures. If our minds are set on the Lord's Word all the time, memorization will be an easy task. While we seize every available opportunity to memorize the Scriptures, the word of Christ will dwell in us richly. If we do not allow the Scriptures to dwell in our heart, it will be hard for the Holy Spirit to speak to us. Whenever God grants us a revelation, He does so through the words of the Bible. If we do not memorize the Scriptures, it will be hard for revelation to come to us. This is the reason we should have God's Word in our mind all the time. Memorizing the Scriptures is not for memorization alone; it is to lay the groundwork for us to receive revelation. If we memorize the Scriptures often and well, it will be easy for us to receive revelation and enlightenment, and the Holy Spirit will find it easier to speak to our spirit. This is the reason we have to spend time to memorize the Word, not just outlines but the actual text. We have to memorize it accurately and carefully.

Besides the above-mentioned crucial passages, other critical portions should also be put together and memorized as a whole. For example, the journey of the Israelites is an important piece of information. The journey which Elisha took when he followed Elijah, the journeys related to Peter's preaching, and the journeys related to Paul's preaching are also important. It is best to memorize all these facts. If we can recall the number of places in Judea and Galilee where the Lord Jesus worked, we will have a clear idea of the Lord's work as a whole in the Gospels. The Lord's work is divided into two sections, the first being carried out in Judea and the second in Galilee. There is also the need to spend some time to memorize the seven feasts and the six offerings in Leviticus. These are basic truths. Once we memorize them, we will realize the riches in God's word. It is not a bad idea to memorize the two prayers of Paul in Ephesians and the ten references to the Holy Spirit in the same book. Verses like these can be found throughout the Bible, and it would do us good to memorize them all. If it is a crucial passage, we should memorize the whole chapter. If it is some isolated verses, we should memorize the verses. We also have to memorize the sixty-six books of the Bible according to the proper order.

### III. BY COMPARING

Searching and memorization alone are not enough. We have to put portions of the Word together and compare them.

In 1 Corinthians 2 Paul speaks of spiritual things and the spiritual man. If we compare the spiritual man with the spiritual things, we will see something.

Psalm 36:9 says, "In Your light we see light." It is not enough to have one kind of light. We need two kinds of light. In fact, one light leads to the other light. Light complements light in the Bible.

Second Peter 1:20 says, "No prophecy of Scripture is of one's own interpretation." It is easy for us to understand this to mean that prophecies are not to be interpreted by man. But according to the grammar of Peter's word, it means that no prophecy is of *its* own interpretation. It is *its* and not *one's*. If this verse meant that no prophecy is to be interpreted by man, Peter would have been too simple, for every Christian knows that God's prophecy cannot be interpreted according to man's own ideas. It would be redundant for Peter to say this. But this was not Peter's meaning. The words *own interpretation* refer to an interpretation of the text by the text itself. When Peter said that no prophecy should be interpreted by its own interpretation, he was saying that each prophecy has a meaning that pertains to that text alone. Yet God's speaking is not completed through just one text. In the books of the prophets we are told that God's word is "here a little, there a little" (Isa. 28:13). Therefore, no Bible student should interpret a passage according to that passage alone. This is to interpret according to its own interpretation. When we read Daniel 9, we should not interpret it merely according to Daniel 9. In reading Revelation 13, we should not interpret it merely according to Revelation 13. If we interpret these two chapters according to just these two chapters, we are interpreting according to their own interpretation, and we are violating the principle of prophetic interpretation.

Here God shows us a principle: We must compare our reading of one passage of the Scriptures with other passages. We cannot base our interpretation on just that text alone. In tackling a teaching found in the Bible, we have to look for explanations of this teaching from other passages of the Bible. This is very important. Many heresies in Christianity have resulted from men holding on to one or two verses of the Bible without consulting other related passages. Satan also quotes the Scriptures here and there, but he quotes them to tempt men. We must remember that the more we compare, the less we will be liable to private interpretation. It is much safer for us to compare one verse with ten other verses. If we can only find five verses, it is better, but not as good as ten verses. The more comparisons we make, the better it is. If there is only one verse that says something, we have to be careful; we cannot build something big upon one isolated instance. Otherwise, we will end up with trouble. It is not very trustworthy to base everything on one verse. In reading the Bible we have to compare. We cannot interpret anything by the text of one passage alone. We must have the confirmation of other passages.

For example, Revelation 19 says that when the Lord descends from heaven to fight, He will remove all His enemies by the sword of His mouth. If we interpret this text by itself, we may conclude that the Lord's mouth contains a sword, and we may even say that this sword is quick, sharp, and shining. If we realize that no Scripture should be interpreted by its own interpretation, we immediately will look for the meaning of "sharp sword" when we come to this passage, and from Ephesians 6:17 we will find that the sharp sword refers to the word of God.

Who do the ten virgins in Matthew 25 refer to? In reading 2 Corinthians 11:2, we find that they refer to the church. (In 2 Corinthians, *virgin* is singular in number, referring to the one church. In Matthew there are ten virgins, which refer to the responsibility of individuals before the Lord. Ten is composed of two fives, and five is the number of human responsibility before God.) Such comparative reading can give us much light.

It is also important to compare the Old Testament with the New Testament. If we compare the scope of God's speaking in the Old Testament with the scope of His speaking in the New Testament, we immediately will see that God's Word is progressive, that the word of revelation is progressive. Some words are found both in the Old Testament and the New Testament. For example, without the book of Daniel, there cannot be the book of Revelation. Yet, in comparison, Revelation is more advanced than the book of Daniel. We can also compare Revelation 2 and 3 with Matthew 13, Revelation 4 and 5 with Philippians 2, and Revelation 6 with Matthew 24. We can also compare the later chapters of Revelation with Daniel. When we compare these passages one with another and interpret one according to the other, we will see many things which we previously have not seen.

We can compare the four Gospels as well. Some things are spoken of in all four Gospels, while other things are not mentioned in any of them. Either case bears much significance. For example, Matthew does not speak of the ascension of the Lord Jesus; it only speaks of His resurrection. Mark speaks of the Lord's ascension. Luke speaks of the Lord's ascension as well as the coming of the Holy Spirit. John does not say anything about the Lord's ascension, but it speaks of

His coming back. The four Gospels all end differently. We have to ask why they are different. If we look for the answer we will see something. Matthew tells us that the Lord is always the King on earth. This is the reason it does not say anything about ascension. Mark speaks of the Lord as God's appointed Servant returning to God. Hence it speaks of ascension. Luke is on the glorified man. Therefore, it speaks about ascension as well as the coming of the Holy Spirit. John says that the Lord is the Only Begotten who is still in heaven and in the Father's bosom. This is the reason it does not speak of ascension. Every book has its own characteristics, and we can only find them by comparison.

### IV. BY MEDITATING

Both Joshua 1:8 and Psalm 1:2 tell us that we have to meditate and dwell on the word of the Lord all the time. At ordinary times (i.e., other than the times when we are reading the Bible), we should meditate on the Lord's Word. We should learn to mold our thoughts according to the thoughts of the Bible. We should be meditating whether or not we are reading the Word. Romans 8:6 speaks of "the mind set on the spirit." This means that we should think of the spirit, set our mind on the spirit, and fix it upon the spirit. This verse does not mean that we should set our mind on the spirit only, but that we should have a mind of the spirit. We should not just concentrate on the spirit, but we should have a concentration that is of the spirit. In other words, whenever our mind turns, it should always turn to God's Word. No matter what the circumstances may be, our mind should always be fixed on God's Word. This is a matter not of artificial reminding but of spontaneous meditating. Ordinarily, our mind should be a mind that is set on the Word. Our mind should not be set on the Bible only when we are thinking about the Bible; it should be on the Bible even when we are not thinking about it. We should be inclined toward God's Word in a spontaneous way.

There are two sides to our meditation. On the one hand, we meditate when we read the Bible. On the other hand, we meditate at all times. When we are reading the Bible, our mind should be meditating on God's Word. But when we are not reading the Bible, we should also be actively exercising ourselves with our trained mind. It is not a matter of forcing ourselves to think about the Scriptures. The Holy Spirit will direct our thoughts in this direction, and it will become part of our habit. Once we develop such a habit, we will spontaneously become rich in the Lord.

# CHAPTER FOUR

# THE PRACTICE
# OF STUDYING THE BIBLE

## I. ALLOCATION OF TIME

Every Bible reader must set aside a certain amount of time every day to study the Bible in a definite way. This should be done apart from his reading during "morning watch." Experience tells us that it is not altogether wise to allocate too much time to such study. When we allocate too much time, we usually cannot keep it up, and the result is not profitable. We should set a standard for ourselves that is reasonable to achieve. Servants of the Lord do not need to spend *more than two hours every day* to study the Bible. Nor should we spend *less than one hour*. Occasionally, when we have more time, we can extend our study to three hours. We have to make a decision about this after careful consideration. Once we have made a decision, we should adhere to it at least for a few years. We should not change our schedule after two or three months. We have to learn to restrict and discipline ourselves a little. Our reading cannot be too capricious. Such free, undisciplined, and "inspirational" reading should not be our pattern. Many people are too careless in their reading. They read a few hours one day and nothing the next day. This shows a lack of perseverance. It is a terrible habit. We should decide on what to do after careful consideration and prayer, and once we have made the decision, we should adhere to it wholeheartedly.

After we have decided to spend, for example, one hour a day on our reading, we should have a plan for that hour. The hour should be divided into several periods, and we should use a different method of study for each period. Some methods are like tree-planting; one does not see the result until eight or ten years later. Other methods are like vegetable farming; one gets a crop every year. The methods that do not reap results for eight or ten years easily discourage a person. This is the reason there is the need for "vegetable farming" methods that reap results in two or three months, methods that will encourage starters to go on. It is easy to get tired if we do the same thing for an hour, and it is easy to give up when we do not see results immediately. This is the reason it is advisable to divide the hour into different periods.

## A. The First Period—for More Serious Subjects

Suppose we have twenty minutes for the first period. These twenty minutes should be devoted to more serious subjects in the Bible. It takes years to reap benefit from this kind of study. Subjects like prophecies, types, and the death of the Lord Jesus require years of study before we can reap results. Studying passages like the sermon on the mount, the prophecy on the Mount of Olives, the parables in Matthew 13, the final discourse of the Lord in the Gospel of John, and teachings concerning the four dispensations will not yield immediate results. We have to spend months and years on them before we will see something. If we want to find something in the Old Testament on these subjects, we must study Genesis and Daniel. We should also read Exodus, Leviticus, and Joshua. If we want to find out more about prophecies, we have to add Zechariah to the list. The first book to study in the New Testament is Matthew, and Romans should be next. Following that we should study Revelation or Hebrews. Then we should study the Gospel of John or the Epistles to the Ephesians or the Galatians. After we finish these books, we will have laid a foundation for ourselves in the New Testament. These studies do not reap benefit immediately; we have to read them dozens of times before we can get something out of them. This kind of study should be done during the first period. During this time our mind is the most clear, and we should tackle the more serious subjects. Of course, I am only giving something in the way of a principle. It depends on each of us as to how we should spend our time specifically.

We should take note of one thing: After studying for twenty minutes, we may be tempted to extend our reading to thirty minutes. We must overcome this temptation. If we have made the decision to read only twenty minutes, we should adhere to twenty minutes. If we can resist extending our time, we will also overcome the temptation of reducing our time from twenty to ten minutes. Once we have made a decision before the Lord, we have to discipline ourselves to adhere to it. We would rather be stuck with something for ten years than be free from it in ten days. We must never be loose or careless. We have to learn to be disciplined.

## B. The Second Period—for Lighter Subjects

During the second twenty minutes, we can turn to lighter subjects, such as the study of specific words. There are at least two to three hundred words in the Bible that need to be studied in depth. For example, the word *blood* is used in the Bible over four hundred times. We should go over all the verses that speak of the blood, note the important ones, and group the ones with similar meanings together. In this way we will compile for ourselves a kind of concordance. This is more meaningful than buying a concordance from a store. It also would be good if we could memorize these verses. Later the Spirit of God may give us revelations. When a revelation comes, we immediately will be able to recall all the verses on the subject. A word such as *calling* was once studied by some brothers, who grouped the verses into ten sections (See heading XXVI in Chapter Five, "Various Plans for Studying the Bible"). We can spend twenty minutes a day studying such words. Twenty minutes is enough for this kind of study. Do not expect to finish a word-study in a day. Some words require two months to finish. The study of the Bible takes time. We cannot be sloppy about it. Otherwise, we will not have the sword of the Spirit but a worthless reed. We have to dive into the Word in a solid way. If our study of the Word is solid, our preaching will also be solid. If our study of the Word is sloppy, our preaching will also be sloppy. Suppose someone comes to us and tells us that the blood can give us a new life. If we have studied the word *blood* carefully, we will know that this teaching is wrong. The life contained in the blood is the life of the soul, not the new life. We have to acquaint ourselves with the fundamental teachings of the whole Bible. Otherwise, we will simply take what others say and be led astray by their mistakes. A knowledge of the fundamental teachings of the whole Bible is not something that comes to us in an instant. We must study each word carefully one by one before we can know what the whole Bible says. Young brothers and sisters have to be conscientious in word-studies. If we can get through several dozen words in a year, we will be able to go through all the important words in the Old and the New Testaments in ten years.

## C. The Third Period—Collecting Facts

In the third period, we should spend ten minutes collecting facts. We have to do this every day. What should we collect? All the metals in the Bible, such as gold, silver, bronze, and iron, have special significance. The precious stones in the Bible also have special significance. We should not consider them as minor issues. They occupy an important role in the interpretation of the Scriptures. Why was the bronze serpent bronze? Why does Revelation 1:15 say that the Lord's feet were "like shining bronze, as having been fired in a furnace"? Why was the head of the image in Nebuchanezzar's dream golden? Why were some of the utensils in the temple golden? Why was the ark covered with gold, not silver? Why were the bases of the tabernacle silver? In Zechariah 5 we find lead. What does this refer to? We have to study these things carefully before we can understand what they mean exegetically. During this period of time, we should collect all these facts and write down the verses one by one. Later, we may devote the first period of time to meditate on them and study them, or we may read about them in the second period. In other words, during the third period, we collect material for our study in the first and second periods. The book of Ephesians speaks of the spirit fifteen times. We can use the third period of time to find these fifteen instances. Ephesians 1:13 speaks of the seal of the Spirit, and we can write down all the verses in the New Testament that speak of the seal.

Ephesians 1:17 speaks of a spirit of wisdom and revelation, and we can write down all the verses that link the spirit with wisdom. After we have collected and sorted out all these facts, we can study them during the twenty minutes of the first or second period. If we do not have the facts gathered and sorted ahead of time, our study will not have a basis and will not be that accurate.

## D. The Fourth Period—Paraphrasing

The fourth period is ten minutes for paraphrasing the Bible. When we have a fresh understanding of a portion of the Word, we should write out the whole portion in simple and intelligible language for the easy comprehension of others. A person who is trained in this exercise will find meaning and significance in every word of the Bible. This requires fine work. It may take a few days to paraphrase one verse. We have to touch the thought of the Holy Spirit with our spirit, and we have to open up ourselves to receive the proper impressions. Our thoughts have to match the thoughts of the writers of the Bible. We have to use basically the same expressions, only with a little more explanation of our own to clarify their meaning.

Paraphrasing should be done paragraph by paragraph. To paraphrase a verse at a time is too little, and to paraphrase a chapter at a time is too much. We should group a few verses together that naturally form a section, read through the whole section, and then paraphrase it verse by verse.

Paraphrasing is different from translation. Translation is brief; it is not detailed enough. Of course, we should not write too much in our paraphrasing, or else we will find ourselves involved in extensive exegesis. Paraphrasing involves a little translation and a little exegesis. It is something that lies between these two things. Exegesis is the exposition of the Bible with our own words, while paraphrasing is the utterance of a passage in the tone of the biblical writers themselves. Translation is a mere rendering of the meaning of the original text, while paraphrasing adds a little of our own explanation to it. Therefore, paraphrasing is a work that lies in between exposition and translation. In paraphrasing we retain the tone of the biblical writers, but here and there we render our own explanations. This kind of paraphrasing helps others to understand words in the Bible that they do not understand. Let us consider a few examples.

Romans 1:1 says, "Paul, a servant of Jesus Christ..." (KJV). We can paraphrase it by saying "Paul, a slave of Jesus Christ." Paul used the word *servant* with the idea that he was the Lord's bondservant, a slave who had no freedom of his own. It is up to us whether or not to interpret the meaning of the word *servant*. But this involves another kind of paraphrasing. Paraphrasing, however, does not have to involve interpretation. If we were trying to interpret this verse, we could write, "I, Paul, was sold to sin. But the blood of the Lord Jesus has purchased me, and now I have become His slave." If we wrote this way, others would be clear about the Lord's right and our consecration. We were sold to sin but the Lord has redeemed us. Now we love to serve Him, we choose to serve Him, and we willingly give ourselves to serve Him. We become His servants on the basis of His purchase and through our choice. When we elaborate on the reason for Paul's being a servant, we make his word crystal clear.

The next phrase says, "Called to be an apostle." It is easy for us to think that Paul was called to *be* an apostle. Actually, this phrase should be translated as "called apostle" or "called as apostle" according to the original language. He was not called to be an apostle; he was a called apostle. In verse 7 we find the same thing: "To all that be in Rome, beloved of God, called to be saints" (KJV). The words *to be* present the same problem. Many people have been believers all their life, yet they still do not regard themselves as saints. According to the original language, the expression should be "called saints." This means that they were called as saints. They were not called to be saints. The word *called* is an adjective, not a verb. It shows us the kind of apostles and the kind of saints that these ones were. It explains a condition, not an action. The advantage of paraphrasing is to discover many biblical truths through the phrases and expressions.

Consider Romans 6:6, which says, "Our old man has been crucified with Him." This verse can be expressed in many different ways. It can be expressed as, "Since my old man has been crucified with Him, I no longer have to be crucified." If our emphasis is on how our old man is crucified *with Him,* we can say, "Because God has placed us in Christ, we are crucified together with Him." This is based on verse 11, which says, "Reckon yourselves to be dead to sin...in Christ Jesus." It is because we are *in* Him that we can be *with* Him. The basis of our being *with* Him is our being *in* Him. Without being *in* Him, we can never be *with* Him. Those who are not *in* Christ cannot be crucified *with* Him. Only those who are *in* Him can be crucified *with* Him. Because God has put us in Christ, we can be crucified with Him. The work of paraphrasing is to make a sentence clear. Every verse has some crucial words, and we must pay attention to these words. If we come across a verse that we do not quite understand, we have to ask the Lord to shine on us so that we can express the verse in language simpler than the original and in utterance more concise than an exegesis. Every time we work on a sentence, we have to ask, "Why is this sentence so difficult to understand?" We have to tackle all the crucial terms in the Bible before we can paraphrase it. For example, if we study the word *crucified* in Greek, we will find that it refers to an accomplished fact. Therefore, we can rewrite this verse: "Our being crucified with Christ is an accomplished fact; it is not an experience that we pursue after." Christ is the One who was crucified. To Him it was an experience, but to us there is no need of an independent crucifixion; we are crucified in Him already. With us this is a fact. Thus, there is more than one way to paraphrase this verse. Everyone has his own way. It all depends on how much one needs clarification or how much others need clarification on a point. Whatever we write, we have to do it in such a way that those who do not understand the verse will understand it.

Consider 1 Corinthians 3:1, which says, "And I, brothers, was not able to speak to you as to spiritual men, but as to fleshy, as to infants in Christ." The word *but* means a great deal here. It means, "You have been believers for all this time. You should know what it means to be spiritual and what it means to be under the discipline of the Holy Spirit. Yet in many things you are still under the influence of the flesh, you still walk by the flesh, and you have not subjected yourselves to the authority of the Spirit. I cannot help *but* to consider you as being fleshy." If we consider for a moment Paul's expression *infants in Christ,* we will realize that Paul was saying, "You have been wasting too much time. It is excusable for a new believer to be under the influence of the flesh. But you have been believers for so many years, and you are still under the power of the flesh. Even today, you are still not grown up in Christ, and I still have to feed you with milk." Whatever our understanding is concerning this passage, we should write it down. In this way, when we read our writing again, we will be clear about the meaning of the passage. If we apply ourselves to this exercise for ten minutes a day, by the time we finish the whole book of 1 Corinthians we will have a good grasp of Paul's thought in writing this Epistle.

The above division of time is a suggestion based on others' experience. In actual practice, everyone can make appropriate arrangements based on his specific needs before God.

## II. TAKING NOTES

While we are reading the Bible, we have to jot down notes. Every student of the Bible has to take notes. We need small notebooks, and we need big notebooks. We should always carry a small notebook in our pocket to jot down our thoughts all the time. We should also jot down our questions. In addition to the small notebook, we should also carry a bigger, consolidated notebook. We should write down systematically in this consolidated book all the things that have passed through our mind and all the materials we have collected. We have to categorize this information for future reference. At the beginning we do not need a detailed division; the categorization can be somewhat general. If we want to categorize our material by theological subjects, we can divide it into five sections, concerning the Father, the Son, the Spirit, the church, and the coming age. It is all right to make finer divisions, but for new believers, these five categories will suffice. Prophecies concerning the church can be grouped under the church. All the doctrines from justification to sanctification also can be grouped under the church. At the beginning we can have five notebooks, one for each of these five categories. When we have more material, we can make further subdivisions.

We must exercise care in taking notes. For example, in reading Romans, we should note that *reign* or *reigning* is used five times in 5:14, 17, and 21. *Much more* is used four times in verses 9, 10, 15, and 17. We have to make a note of all of these. Mark 13:9 says, "For My sake," verse 13 says, "On account of My name," and verse 20 says, "On account of the chosen." Why do these three verses say these three different things? Consider the example of Matthew 24 and 25. How many questions did the disciples ask the Lord on the Mount of Olives? How many verses answer one question, how many answer another? The disciples were limited in their knowledge. Their questions were not that pertinent. This is the reason not much is recorded concerning their questions. But the Lord Jesus spoke a great deal in His answers. We have to pay attention to this speaking and find out from which verse to which verse are Jesus' answers and from which verse to which verse are His additional words. In this way, we will have a thorough grasp of the whole prophecy on the Mount of Olives. Consider the three occurrences of "I said" in Isaiah 6:5, 8, and 11. The first "I said" is a confession, the second "I said" is a consecration, while the third "I said" is a fellowship. We have to take note of all of these. This kind of material is very useful to us as well as to other brothers and sisters. All good readers of the Bible are diligent. They do not become good by accident.

### III. TOOLS

Studying the Bible is like working at a trade; we have to have the proper tools.

### A. The Bible

We should have two large-print Bibles for our own reading. We also should have a small-print Bible for our travel and for meeting. If we cannot have two Bibles for our own reading, we should at least have one. The print should not be too small, because if it is too small, it will be easy to miss the meanings

in the words. The font must at least be size five. Preferably it
should be size four or three. Size two is too large, and it is
suitable only for elderly ones. [Translator's note: These sizes
refer to Chinese typesetting conventions, with the higher the
size, the smaller the print. The English equivalent of size five
is approximately nine points, and the equivalent of size two is
approximately twenty-four points.] It is best to have two Bibles
for studying. In one of them we can put marks and notes. The
other should be left unmarked. By reading an unmarked Bible,
we will not be affected by our previous readings, and every
time we read a passage, it will be like reading it for the first
time. The other Bible should be used for marking and under-
lining. We can write notes, underline and circle words, or link
similar passages together. But we should not spend too much
time or be too detailed in doing this. For our daily spiritual
nourishment, we can use the unmarked Bible. For research,
we can use the marked Bible.

The Chinese Union Version is the best Chinese translation
of the Bible. It is also one of the best translations of the Bible
in the world available today. One of the reasons for this is
that it is based on the best edition of the Greek text. This
translation is very accurate in many places, even more
accurate than the King James Version. For example, the King
James Version in many instances does not distinguish between
"Jesus Christ" and "Christ Jesus." But the Chinese Union
Version is always accurate in the order of the two expressions.
It is good to buy several different translations and compare
them. Another good translation is the Wen-li (classical) Union
Version. In many instances, its monosyllabic terms are better
than those used in the Chinese Union Version. The vernacular
Chinese language does not express itself as well as the
classical Chinese language when it comes to terminology. For
example, both "making alive" and "raising up" are translated
as *fu-hwo* in vernacular Chinese. But the classical Chinese
makes a distinction between the two. One is *fu-chi* and the
other is *fu-hwo*. In some cases the vernacular Chinese is more
restricted than the classical Chinese, and in some other cases,
the opposite is true. Another version worth considering is the
Joseph (?) Version. He was a Jew, and after he became a

Christian, he felt the need to translate the Bible into Chinese. For that very purpose he studied Chinese and later did a translation all by himself. We can also compare the New Testament translation of the "Shin-Ju-Ku" Version. The Christian Gospel Bookroom has also done a translation of the Gospel of Matthew. It can be used for reference as well. The most reliable versions, however, are still the Chinese Union Version and the Wen-li Union Version. If a person can read English, he can also try to have a copy of Darby's translation.

## B. Concordances

Other than the Bible, one should also have a concordance. Courtenay H. Fenn's compilation is probably one of the better ones. Yet even this one is not too complete. In the future we hope to publish a concordance according to the original Greek. The Lord willing, we will publish an Old Testament concordance as well.

## C. Bible Dictionaries

In addition to the above tools, we should also have Bible dictionaries. For example, we need a dictionary to tell us the meaning of *Urim* and *Thummim,* the histories of the six Marys, etc. A dictionary can give us all this information. But we should use a dictionary whose doctrinal conviction is sound. One can consult the *Bible Encyclopedia* by Ou-Er. This can be considered a Bible dictionary. Unfortunately, its Chinese version is out of print. Perhaps one can still find a copy of it in the library or in old bookstores.

## D. Outlines of the Bible

We need another book to help us make good outlines of the Bible. We can consult *Once a Year through the Bible* (see Volume 2 of *The Collected Works*). This book has good outlines. Many Christians all over the world have used the divisions outlined in this book for their study of the Bible.

These reference books are useful to us in our study of the Bible. They are indispensable tools.

# CHAPTER FIVE

# VARIOUS PLANS FOR STUDYING THE BIBLE

The Bible is an extraordinary book. It includes sixty-six books and is authored by thirty-nine to forty people. The content is extremely rich. To read this book, we must have a plan. Without a plan, we cannot reap great benefit from our reading. From different sources, we have gathered twenty-eight different plans for studying the Scriptures. If we have time, we can try all of these plans one by one. More elderly brothers may choose only a few.

## I. MAIN CHARACTERS

There are many characters in the Old Testament, such as Adam, Abel, Noah, Abraham, Isaac, Jacob, Moses, Joshua, David, and Solomon. We have to study the history of these men carefully. We should learn their history not only from the Old Testament but from the New Testament as well.

The common impression is that Adam's history is found only in chapters two and three of Genesis. But upon careful reading, we find that the books of Romans and 1 Corinthians also speak about Adam, and what they say is quite crucial. More about Adam can also be found in Ephesians 5. In studying Adam's history, we have to know about his place in God's plan, his creation, his initial innocence and sinlessness, his relationship with Eve, his judgment from God and the promise he received from God after the fall, his expulsion from the garden of Eden, his life outside Eden, and finally, his relation to the last Adam. If we spend three or four months to study him in detail, we will understand many fundamental issues in the Bible.

After we are finished with Adam's history, we can go on to Abel's history. We should read his history not only in

Genesis but also in Hebrews 11. We have to go through all the passages in the Bible that speak of Abel in order to find the basic message that God has for us through him. What is the reason behind God's acceptance of Abel and rejection of Cain? Many people think that Abel's sacrifice was accepted because it had blood. But this is too heavily biased toward the New Testament; it does not bring out the root cause of God's acceptance of Abel's sacrifice. Man's responsibility in the garden of Eden was to dress and keep it. After man sinned, he could till the ground for his sustenance, but in his sinful state it was wrong to offer a sacrifice to God of his sustenance. Cain offered the produce of the land to God, as if he had forgotten the fall of sin. This was the reason his offering was not accepted. If a child commits a great offense and yet approaches his parents as if nothing has happened, he cannot possibly be approved. God cannot be pleased with sinners who nonchalantly act as if nothing has happened. The problem with Cain was that he acted as if nothing had happened, even though he had sinned. Abel, however, acknowledged the fact of sin. At that time men did not raise sheep for food. Only after the flood did men begin to take meat (Gen. 9:3). The purpose of keeping sheep was strictly for offering them as sacrifices to God. The sheep were killed and their skin was used for covering (3:21). God requires man to acknowledge that he is a sinner. Abel came to God according to this requirement, and God accepted him.

We can go on with the history of Noah and the history of Abraham, Isaac, Jacob, etc. in the same way.

## II. WOMEN

Women occupy a specific line in the Bible. We can study all the women as one category. We can study Eve and find out about her creation, her words, her independent acts, her fall and punishment, and her promise from God to be the mother of all living. We can go on to Sarah, Rebekah, Tamar, Ruth, Rahab, Hannah, Abigail, the Shulamite, etc. We can continue with the woman with man-child in Revelation 12, the great harlot in chapter seventeen, and the Lamb's wife in chapter nineteen. We can see a clear line here. All the women in the Bible, positively or negatively, typify the many aspects of one woman—the church.

### III. TYPES

In order to study the types in the Old Testament, we must first have a foundation of the New Testament. The New Testament speaks of Christ, His redemption, the church, and the Holy Spirit. These are four great spiritual things. The chief types in the Old Testament are types of these four things. They either typify Christ, redemption, the church, or the Holy Spirit. In the Old Testament we see the photograph before we see the person. In the New Testament we first see the person, and then we go back to the Old Testament to see the photograph. If we have seen the reality of Christ, redemption, the church, and the Holy Spirit, it is much easier for us to see the Old Testament types.

The re-creation in Genesis 1 is a type of the new creation. In chapter two Eve is a type of the church in its sinless state. When we think of ourselves, we think of sin because we are inseparably linked to sin. Yet God shows us that the relationship between Christ and the church is apart from sin, for their relationship began in Genesis 2 not Genesis 3. Adam was related to Eve in Genesis 2. Hence, their relationship had nothing to do with sin, even as Christ and the church have nothing to do with sin. When we think of the church, we should never think of sin. In God's eyes the church has no sin. The Lord Jesus' death for the sinner was for the remission of sin. But His death for the church was not for sin but for life. In Genesis 3 we see the fig leaves and the skins of animals. In chapter four we see the offerings. Later, we see Isaac. Who is Isaac? Is he a type of the church, the Holy Spirit, redemption, or the Lord Jesus? In reading the New Testament, we can see that Isaac somewhat typifies the Lord Jesus. Isaac was not only born of Abraham or Sarah; he was born of promise. Hence, Isaac somewhat resembles the Lord Jesus. To Sarah, Isaac was his father's only begotten son. This again resembles the Lord Jesus. To Abraham, everything that Isaac had was inherited; Isaac simply enjoyed his inheritance. In this respect he indeed resembles the Lord

Jesus. God sent the Holy Spirit to the world. The Spirit secured the church and espoused it to Christ as the Lamb's wife. Isaac's father sent his old servant to his own country and tribe to find a woman, Rebekah, to be Isaac's wife. There is a correspondence here. If we compare the Old Testament and the New Testament, we can find many things in the New Testament that match the Old Testament types. In Galatians, Isaac typifies the spiritual Christians. Ishmael typifies a fleshly walk in the church, while Isaac typifies a spiritual walk. Ishmael was begotten by Abraham through Hagar, that is, through the flesh. He typifies man's own work. Isaac was born after Abraham gave up any hope of a child being born; he was born of God's promise. Hence, he typifies the work of the Holy Spirit. This is just one example of types. If we go through the Bible chapter by chapter, we will find many different types. The book that provides the most types is Genesis. We can say that Genesis is the nursery from which the seedlings of the whole Bible grow.

The whole book of Exodus is a type of our salvation from the world. The Passover is a type of the breaking of bread. The crossing of the Red Sea is a type of baptism. The murmuring and sojourning in the wilderness are types of God's children in their various conditions. The living water is a type of the Holy Spirit.

The tabernacle is a type of our Lord Jesus while He sojourned on the earth. It is also a type of our sojourn in the world. The tabernacle did not have a floor, and it was pitched in the wilderness. We have to wait until the New Jerusalem before we will see the streets of gold. While we are passing through this world, we have a glorious fellowship with the Lord. God's goal for us is Canaan; He does not want us to remain in the wilderness.

Further on, we see in the book of Numbers that the Israelites passed through forty-two stations after their exodus from Egypt prior to their entry into Canaan. Every station has its significance. In reading the names of the stations we get a picture of man's sojourning as well the condition for his entry into Canaan.

The offerings, feasts, and ordinances regarding cleansing are all types, and we have to study them.

The book of Joshua is a book with profound types. I am not saying that all the types in this book are profound. I am saying that there are many profound things in the book of Joshua. In order to understand the significance of the Israelites entering Canaan and the warfare in Canaan, we must first know what Canaan typifies. Some think that Canaan typifies heaven. But if Canaan typifies heaven, will there be warfare in heaven? If we are careful in our reading, we will conclude that Canaan cannot be a type of heaven. It is a type of our heavenly position. It is the equivalent of the heavenlies spoken of in Ephesians. On the one hand, we are seated with Christ in the heavenlies. On the other hand, we wrestle against the spiritual forces of evil in the heavenlies (Eph. 6:12). In studying this typology, we must not stop with the book of Joshua; we must also study Ephesians. In fact, Joshua must be read not only with Ephesians but with Hebrews as well. The entrance into Canaan in the book of Joshua typifies two things: spiritual warfare (in Ephesians) and rest (in Hebrews). The rest here clearly refers to the kingdom. Hence, Canaan is not a type of heaven but a type of the kingdom rest. Not everyone who passed under the blood of the lamb or ate of the Passover lamb entered Canaan; only two entered. The rest died in the wilderness. Many are called but few are chosen. Hence, Canaan is a type of the kingdom. The entrance into Canaan typifies our reigning in the kingdom. Once we are clear about this fundamental point, we will see which part of Joshua is a type of a Christian's position in the heavenlies today and which part is a type of his reward in the future.

The many lawless acts in the book of Judges typify man's self-willed life which results in all kinds of confusion.

In Samuel we see man's reign and God's entrusting of His authority to man. Before a man after God's heart was raised up, a man after man's heart stepped in. David was a man after God's heart, but before him, a man after man's heart, Saul, came. It is clear that Saul typifies the reign of antichrist. We see how the king after God's choice went into battle and how he enjoyed peace. We see the battles of David and the glory of Solomon. The reign of Saul typifies the condition during the great tribulation, the reign of David typifies the condition after the tribulation, and the reign of Solomon typifies the millennium. All of these are clear types.

Solomon's building of the temple is again a type of Christ building the church. The temple was in Jerusalem, typifying the church meeting and worshipping in the Lord's name, because God placed His name in Jerusalem. Jerusalem was the only place which God recognized and in which He put His own name (1 Kings 14:21). When Jeroboam rose up, he set up altars in Bethel and Dan for worship, and God condemned this. God wants man to worship only at the place where His name is established. He does not want man to worship anywhere else. During times of revival, the kings removed the altars. But some kings did not remove them. This is a type of the many revivals that have taken place in the church. Later, the temple was destroyed; this is a type of the church becoming desolated. Afterwards, Nehemiah, Zechariah, and Zerubbabel returned to rebuild the temple. Although the rebuilt temple was not as glorious as the one that had been destroyed, there was a beginning of recovery back to the original ground. This is a type of the recovery of the church. This recovery will be completed at the Lord's second coming. Then the church will be a glorious church.

## IV. PROPHECIES

One third of the whole Bible contains prophecies. We can classify the prophecies in the Bible into two categories, those concerning Christ's first coming and those concerning His second coming. Prophecies concerning His first coming can be found in the Pentateuch, the Psalms, and the books of the prophets. The Lord Jesus has come, and it seems as if prophecies concerning His first coming are not very exciting. However, in order to study prophecy, we must pay attention to the Lord's first coming. We have to find all the prophecies in the Old and New Testaments about His first coming and write them down because this will teach us something concerning the principle of prophecies. The prophecies concerning

His second coming will be fulfilled the same way as the prophecies concerning His first coming.

There are rules for exposition of everything spoken of in the Bible. Anything that should be interpreted spiritually is clearly indicated by the text of the Scriptures itself. For example, Revelation 1 speaks of the seven stars in the right hand of the Lord as the messengers of the seven churches. This should not be interpreted literally, and the text tells us this. The seven lampstands, which the Lord walked in the midst of, refer to the churches. This is also clearly stated in the text. Every type should be interpreted spiritually. In type, Adam does not refer to Adam literally, but to Christ, and Eve does not refer to Eve literally, but to the church. However, prophecies can be interpreted according to two different, basic principles. They can be interpreted spiritually, in which case the fulfillment is a fulfillment in meaning only, or they can be interpreted literally, in which case the fulfillment is literal. For example, Matthew 2:17-18 says, "At that time what was spoken through Jeremiah the prophet was fulfilled, saying, 'A voice in Ramah was heard, weeping and great lamentation: Rachel weeping for her children, and she would not be comforted, because they are no more.'" This is a fulfillment in meaning. Consider the example of Acts 2:16, which says, "But this is what is spoken through the prophet Joel." The condition that was seen at Pentecost was like the one described in the book of Joel. This is also a fulfillment in meaning. As to the first coming of the Lord Jesus, many prophecies were fulfilled literally. The virgin literally referred to a virgin. Egypt literally referred to Egypt. Not having a single bone broken meant exactly that. They were all literally fulfilled. Since many of the fulfillments concerning the Lord's first coming were literal, most of the fulfillments concerning His second coming will be literal as well.

Some prophecies concern the Jews, others concern the Gentiles, and still others concern the church. These three kinds of prophecies are all different. Most of Moses' and Balaam's prophecies concerned the Jews. Of course, we find many prophecies concerning the Jews in the books of the prophets also. Prophecies concerning the Gentiles can be found

in the book of Daniel. We should also pay attention to what
the Lord Jesus said on earth in Matthew 24. Revelation 8—11,
13, 15—16, and 18 are all prophecies concerning the Gentiles.
Prophecies concerning the church can be found in such
chapters as Matthew 13, Revelation 2—3, 12, 14—15, 1 Corinthians 15, and 1 Thessalonians 4. We have to know clearly
which prophecies pertain to the Jews, which to the Gentiles,
and which to the church.

Prophecies concerning the Jews can be divided into two
main branches: those concerning the day of the Lord and
those concerning the earthly blessings in the kingdom.

With regard to the prophecies concerning the Gentiles, we
have to pay particular attention to all the prophecies uttered
during "the times of the Gentiles" after the destruction of
the Jewish nation. Chapters such as Daniel 2, 4, and 7, the
seventy weeks in chapter nine, and everything thereafter,
including the book of Revelation, contain prophecies for the
Gentiles. Simply put, these prophecies first depict the period
from the destruction of the Jewish nation to the end time,
which covers the entire history spanned in the great image
of Daniel 2. Second, they speak of the ten horns (the ten
kings) in the end time, the other horn (the other king), and
the antichrist. Third, they speak of the blessings enjoyed by
the Gentiles in the millennium.

Concerning the church, there are the prophecies depicting
the two thousand years of church history, the rapture, the
judgment seat, the kingdom, and eternity.

## V. DISPENSATIONS

God deals with man according to dispensations. In every
age God has His own way of dealing with man. In one
dispensation He deals with man one way. In another dispensation He deals with man another way. In one dispensation
man is saved through one means. In another dispensation he
is saved through another means. In one dispensation God has
one kind of requirement for man's conduct. In another dispensation He has another kind of requirement for man's
conduct. If we are not clear about the different dispensations,
we will think that some statements in the Bible are confusing.

But once we distinguish between the dispensations, the confusion will disappear.

Some expositors have divided history into seven dispensations. But according to the Bible itself, there should only be four dispensations. The first is the dispensation of the patriarchs. This dispensation began with Adam because Romans 5:14 clearly says, "From Adam until Moses." Although there were many fine differences within this period, on the whole, it was "from Adam until Moses." This is the first dispensation. The second is the dispensation of the law, which spans from Moses to Christ. But at which point in the history of Christ did this dispensation end? The Lord Jesus said that the law and the prophets ended with John (Matt. 11:13; Luke 16:16). He meant that this dispensation ended with John. The third dispensation is the dispensation of grace, which spans the time from the first coming of Christ to His second coming (Acts 3:20-21). Although the Lord still cares for the Jews during this period, the focus of His attention is on the Gentiles. We are in the dispensation of grace. The fourth dispensation is the kingdom, which spans the time from the second coming of Christ to the end of the kingdom age (Rev. 20).

In every dispensation we have to pay attention to man's original position, his responsibilities, his failures, and God's way of dealing with him. After we study these points carefully, it will be easy for us to solve all of the seemingly contradictory problems.

## VI. TOPICS

The Bible contains many topics, including: 1) creation, 2) man, 3) angels, 4) sin, 5) the satanic kingdom, 6) salvation, 7) repentance, 8) the person of Christ, 9) the work of Christ, 10) the life of Christ, 11) the Holy Spirit, 12) regeneration, 13) eternal life, 14) eternal security, 15) sanctification, 16) justification, 17) selection, 18) forgiveness, 19) righteousness, 20) freedom, 21) law, 22) inspiration, 23) revelation, 24) the Body of Christ, 25) ministers of the word, 26) God's authority, 27) the second coming of Christ, 28) judgment, 29) the kingdom, 30) eternity, etc. At the beginning we can study one topic a year. After a while we can study two topics a year, and later, even four topics a year.

For example, the person of Christ is a big topic. How should we begin such a study? We can divide this topic according to the following subtopics: 1) He is God. As God, He has the aspect of being the Word as well as the aspect of being the Son of God. 2) He is man. This relates to how He became Jesus and how He expresses Himself as a man. 3) He is both God and man. He slept in the boat; this shows that He is a man. Yet He woke up to rebuke the wind and the waves; this shows that He is God. He attended the wedding feast; this shows that He is a man. But at the feast He changed water into wine; this shows that He is God. He asked for water from the Samaritan woman; this shows that He is a man. Yet He explained to her about the living water; this shows that He is God. 4) His history. This refers to His living on earth. 5) His position today, that is, His position after His ascension. 6) His future position, that is, His place in glory when He comes again.

We can also classify the work of Christ into different categories: 1) The relationship between His person and His work, 2) His substitution, 3) His satisfaction of God's requirement for the redemption of sin, 4) His reconciliation of men to God, 5) His acceptance and receiving of men, 6) His priesthood, and 7) His mediatorial work.

The life of Christ can be classified under the following categories: 1) His birth, 2) His death, 3) His resurrection, 4) His ascension, and 5) His coming again. In speaking of His birth, we have to see what incarnation is. The crystallized view of His incarnation is that everything abstract and divine has become concrete and human. What is God's patience? We do not know what it is, and we cannot know what it is. But the Lord Jesus has come. This is not only the Word becoming flesh, but Patience becoming flesh. The abstract and invisible Patience has now become tangible. The principle of incarnation is the principle of Love becoming flesh, Holiness becoming flesh, Joy, Obedience, etc. becoming flesh. In other words, what was intangible as God's virtues have now become tangible. When God became a man, the abstract became tangible.

Jesus is the standard man that God is after. We cannot come up to God's standard. This is the reason we cannot draw near to God. A veil was present, and the more beautiful the veil looked, the harder it was for man to enter in. But thank God that death has come in. What is the meaning of death? On the one hand, it means redemption; and on the other hand, it means the termination of everything of the old creation. Death is the end of the old creation, and the death of Christ is the end of the whole creation. The veil was split from top to bottom; this is death. After this, there is resurrection, which is a new beginning. It is God's creation. It is the new life, and this life is not bound by death. Death cannot hold this life or keep it from coming alive. It does not have that power. Resurrection means the passing away of death and trials; it is a vindication of His power. Then there is the ascension, which is victory over Satan positionally. Satan is under us. Christ's ascension has put us on the same ground as Himself. We now enjoy His victory. The Lord's coming again is the manifestation of the dawning of a new order of authority. Simply put, incarnation speaks of God's standard. Death speaks of the termination of the old creation which has fallen short of God's standard. Resurrection speaks of a new beginning, while ascension speaks of a new position. His coming again is His manifestation in glory. How precious are all these things in the eyes of God!

## VII. GOD'S RELATIONSHIP WITH MAN

Some have classified God's relationship with man in the Bible according to the following considerations: 1) God, 2) men in general, that is, humanity in general, 3) the individual, 4) the God-man, 5) God and man, 6) God in man, and 7) God over men. This is a good division. First, we have God; this is clear enough. Second, we have all men, that is, humanity. This includes Adam's fall and sin and everything that is in Adam. Third, we have the individual, which includes individual sin and individual judgment. Fourth, we have the God-man, which we see in the Gospels; the Lord Jesus is the God-man. Fifth, we have God and man, which involves the truth of the gospel preached in the Epistles. Sixth, we have God in man, which points to all of God's operations within man, involving the deeper truths in the Epistles. Seventh, we have God over men, which refers the kingdom age, when God will be King over all men. This includes all future events. We can adopt this plan and write down all the subjects in seven different notebooks.

### VIII. CHRONOLOGY

The study of biblical chronology may not reap much immediate benefit. But at least it will help the reader to develop a careful habit in reading the Word. The Bible contains clear records of chronology. One can calculate the exact number of years from man's creation to the birth of Jesus. From Adam to the flood is clearly 1,656 years. The Bible clearly gives us a record of the number of years for each period of history. Thus, we know the number of years from the time of the exodus to the entrance into Canaan. We know the number of years the Israelites lived under the judges, the number of years they lived under the kings, and the number of years from that time until the time of Daniel and from then to the time of the Lord Jesus. Some numbers are found in Stephen's words. We even find a record of the number of years a certain person slept on his right and the number of years he slept on his left (Ezek. 4:4-6). From the time of the rebuilding of Jerusalem to the coming of the Lord Jesus was sixty-nine weeks (483 years). In this way, we can trace the number of years all the way from Adam to the Lord Jesus. Beginning from Genesis God has laid down a chronology, and this chronology has never been interrupted. In order to study the Bible, we have to learn to be a careful and attentive person.

In studying chronology we can discover things we ordinarily would not discover. For example, when we study the history of the patriarchs, we find that Adam was still alive at the time Enoch was walking on the earth. Adam had seen God, but Enoch had never seen God. We may think that the one who had seen God should have been raptured. But in the end Enoch was raptured; Adam was not raptured. This is a lesson to us. Further along we find the name Methuselah, which means "when he dies, something will happen." In the year that Methuselah died, the flood came. This also shows the accuracy of the Bible.

Paul tells us in Galatians 3 that grace preceded the law; it did not come after the law. We have to know the chronology, and then we will see that the grace of promise was in existence 430 years before the coming of the law.

It is easy to find biblical chronology from the book of Genesis. After Genesis it is more difficult to dig out the chronology. Yet the difficulty lies only in man's reluctance to study the Word. How many years are there from Israel's exodus out of Egypt to Solomon's building of the temple? First Kings 6:1 says, "Then in the four hundred eightieth year after the children of Israel had come forth out of the land of Egypt, in the fourth year of his reign over Israel, in the month of Ziv (this is the second month), Solomon began to build the house of Jehovah." Yet Acts 13:18-22 says, "And for a time of about forty years He carried them as a nurse in the wilderness....And after these things, for about four hundred and fifty years, He gave them judges until Samuel the prophet. And afterward...God gave them Saul...for forty years. And when He had deposed him, He raised up David for them as king." All these years added together equal 530 years. When David's reign of forty years (1 Kings 2:11) and the three years of Solomon's reign before he built the temple are also added, the number of years comes to 573. Hence the record of 1 Kings has ninety-three fewer years than the record of Acts 13. What is the reason for this difference? According to the record of Judges, the children of Israel were taken captive five times. The first lasted eight years (3:8), the second eighteen years (v. 14), the third twenty years (4:2-3), the fourth seven years (6:1), and the last forty years (13:1). All of these years added together equal exactly ninety-three years. It seems that 1 Kings is short of ninety-three years. Actually, it purposely deleted the years of captivity. There is a need of the supplement of the record of Judges. The records of the Bible are like a chain; no link in the chain can be missing. Every link has to be present. God Himself has put these links together, and all we have to do is find the links.

Hence, the study of chronology is very useful in training us to be accurate.

## IX. NUMBERS

Many numbers in the Bible have significance. The following are some examples.

One signifies the one unique God.

Two signifies fellowship.

Three also signifies God because He is triune. One refers to God's unity, and three refers to God's completion.

Four is the first number that is built upon three. It is three plus one. Hence, four is the number of creation. Everything that relates to the creature is four in number. For example, there are four corners of the earth, four seasons, four winds, and four rivers that flow from the garden of Eden. The image in Nebuchadnezzar's dream has four sections. Four beasts come out of the sea. The living creatures that represent all creation are four in number. The Lord Jesus' life on earth is recorded in four Gospels. Everything that is produced from God is four in number.

Five is the number of man's separation. The left hand has five fingers. So does the right hand. Of the ten virgins five are foolish and five wise. Five also signifies human responsibility before God. The ear is one of the five organs, the thumb is one of the five fingers, and the big toe is one of the five toes. Applying the blood to the right ear, the thumb of the right hand, and the big toe of the right foot signifies man's separation to bear responsibility before God.

Six is man's number. Man was created on the sixth day. Seven is the number of perfection. Six is less than seven. This means that what man does can never match what God does.

Seven is the number of perfection. This perfection refers to the present temporary perfection; it is not eternal perfection. Three is the number of God. Four is the number of the creature. The sum of the Creator with the creature is perfection. God plus man equals perfection. But this is only three plus four; it is a temporary perfection. Everything temporal in the Bible is signified by seven. For example, there are seven days to a week, seven parables in Matthew 13, seven churches in Revelation, seven lampstands, seven messengers, seven seals, seven trumpets, and seven bowls. All these refer to temporal perfection rather than perfection in eternity.

Eight is the number of resurrection. Seven is a cycle. Eight is the first number after seven. The Lord Jesus resurrected on the eighth day. Hence, eight is the number of resurrection.

Nine is three times three, a multiplicity of God's number. God's testimony is not only God's word but God's speaking to us.

Ten signifies human perfection. The human number is completed at ten. For example, there are ten fingers to the hands and ten toes to the feet.

Eleven does not have much significance in the Bible.

Twelve is also a number for perfection, but this perfection refers to the perfection in eternity. There are two numbers for perfection: seven and twelve. Seven is divine perfection and has to do with today. Twelve is also divine perfection, but it has to do with eternity. The interesting thing is that in the new heaven and new earth, the number seven will be gone. The New Jerusalem has twelve gates, twelve foundations, the names of the twelve apostles, twelve kinds of precious stones, and twelve pearls. The wall of the city was a hundred and forty-four cubits, which is twelve times twelve. All these will remain forever. Thus, twelve signifies eternal perfection. Why is seven temporal perfection and twelve eternal perfection? Three plus four is simply God plus man, the Creator plus the creature. But three times four is the Creator multiplied by the creature. This means that the two are mingled together. There is a difference between addition and multiplication. In multiplication, God and man are no longer separate. It is a oneness between the creating God and the created beings. Such a oneness is eternal. Hence, the perfection signified by twelve is an eternal perfection.

## X. PARABLES

We can go through all the parables of the Bible. After studying a few of them carefully, we will realize that there are certain principles to interpreting parables. One cannot interpret them in any way he chooses. Once we identify principles, we will know how to interpret other parables when we study them.

Every parable has its subject and its subsidiary points. In interpreting a parable, one must distinguish between the main thought and the subsidiary thought. The main subject must be interpreted point by point. Subsidiary thoughts can be interpreted in detail, or they can be skipped over. For example, the Lord spoke seven parables in Matthew 13, the first of which is the parable of the sower. There is one kind of seed but four kinds of ground. The word is the same, but the hearts are different. This is the subject. We have to pay attention to the word and the four kinds of hearts. Other points, such as the meaning of the devouring of the seed by the birds or the significance of the number of "folds" the good seed multiplies, are not as crucial. Some seeds can multiply a thousandfold or even twelve hundredfold. But the Lord does not say anything about them. This means that the exact number of "folds" is not important. If we pay attention to the size of the birds, the altitude they are flying, or the exact number of "folds" the seeds multiply, we are on the wrong track. In interpreting parables, the first thing to do is distinguish the subject from the subsidiary points.

Another point worth noting is that no parable is to be interpreted in a literal way. For example, in the parable of the sower, the sower does not mean an actual sower, the field does not mean an actual field, and the seed is not an actual seed. This is obvious. All parables have their spiritual significance and should be interpreted spiritually. But this does not mean that every point within a parable has to have spiritual significance attached to it. It only means that the main points in the parable must be interpreted spiritually. The subsidiary points can be interpreted literally. Some people try to attach interpretation to every main point as well as every minor point in a parable. This is wrong. Matthew 13 is the first instance where the Lord spoke to us in parables, and in the first parable the Lord gave us the interpretation Himself. He did not interpret every point. With some points, He gave the interpretations. With other points,

He did not interpret at all. For example, in expounding the "good earth," He told us that the earth refers to man's heart, while good refers to the state of being noble and good (Luke 8:15). The Lord has interpreted this for us. We know that a noble and good heart is the subject here. The Lord did not expand on the meaning of the words "yielded fruit." Hence, the yielding of fruit is not the main thought. If we are caught up with the details, we will lose sight of the spiritual significance of the passage, and our course will be wrong. It is not easy to interpret the parables. One must seek light concerning each one of them before he can interpret them properly.

### XI. MIRACLES

We should pay particular attention to the miracles of the Lord Jesus. One can, of course, also study the other miracles. For the Old Testament miracles, one can study those of Elijah and Elisha. For the New Testament miracles, one can study those of Paul's. If we consider the miracles as a special subject and study them, we will find out that each miracle has its own characteristics. For example, there is a difference between the miracle of healing the blind and the miracle of healing the lame. The eyes have to do with seeing; the blind have to see. Lameness has to do with power; the lame have to walk. In studying these miracles, we must first find out the special characteristics in each case and then find out how the Lord deals with them. This will give us a glimpse as to how He deals with our spiritual problems.

The Lord attached a spiritual teaching to some miracles. For example, in the case of the man born blind in John 9, the Lord clearly said that He would make the blind see and those that can see blind (v. 39). Again, in the case of the resurrection of Lazarus, the Lord clearly said that He is the resurrection and the life (11:25).

Some miracles are not followed explicitly by the Lord's teachings. Yet there are teachings contained in the miracles, and we have to look to the Lord to show us these teachings. For example, in the case of the healing of the lame man, there is spiritual teaching attached to it. At the time the

Lord healed him, He said, "Your sins are forgiven." But He did not simply forgive his sins; He also said to him, "Rise, take up your mat and go to your house." The man rose up, took up the mat, and went out before all men (Mark 2:3-12). Here we find a spiritual principle: It is not enough to be forgiven of our sins; we must have the manifestation of the signs of life and the ability to walk spiritually. No one can say that he is forgiven who cannot rise up to walk. Those who are forgiven will surely walk. Forgiveness comes before walking, and walking is the result of forgiveness. We see a very clear picture here.

## XII. THE LORD'S TEACHINGS ON EARTH

We can study all the teachings that the Lord taught, including Matthew 5, 6, 7, 13, 24, 25. The Gospels of Luke and John also contain many of the Lord's teachings. John 14, 15, and 16 are also important chapters on the Lord's teachings. When we read them we have to pay attention to where the Lord was speaking. Did He teach them in the land of Judea or in Galilee? Was He speaking to the disciples or to the crowd? Was He speaking to both groups or only to the disciples and not to the crowd? If we study the teachings this way, we will grasp the central messages. If we want to work for the Lord, at least we have to study His parables, miracles, and teachings. Otherwise, we will have no material to work on. Our hands will be too empty, and we will not be able to meet the needs.

## XIII. COMPARING THE FOUR GOSPELS

This is also an important way to study the Bible. Why did the Spirit not write one complete gospel, but instead chose to write four different Gospels? Why are the records in the four Gospels seemingly different at times and the sequence of events rearranged? Sometimes the numbers even do not agree. If we do not study them carefully, we will not realize the wonder behind the Spirit's inspiration.

In reading the four Gospels, the first thing we have to do is subdivide them into sections. The subdivision must be detailed. We can set aside a bigger notebook and write down all the events of the four Gospels in it under four columns.

For example, in recording the genealogy of the Lord, we can put Matthew 1:1-17 in the first column and Luke 3:23-38 in the third column. Mark and John do not have a genealogy, so we can leave the second and fourth columns empty. Some events are recorded in only one Gospel, while others are recorded in all four Gospels. After we finish this work, we can turn to our notebook and everything will become clear. If we further compare all the entries in the columns, we will find the similarities and differences between these records. Such comparative reading will reveal many places that differ, and these differences will reveal to us the sovereign arrangements of the Holy Spirit.

The genealogy in Matthew is divided into three groups of fourteen generations: From Abraham to David, from David to the captivity into Babylon, and from the captivity to Christ. The genealogy in Luke traces backward. Matthew goes from Abraham to David, while Luke goes from David to Abraham. Matthew goes from David to the captivity in Babylon, while Luke goes from Salathiel back to David. Matthew goes from Abraham to his descendants, while Luke goes from Abraham back to Adam. Therefore, if Matthew's genealogy is in three sections, Luke's genealogy should be in four sections. Luke's genealogy begins with Mary, and Matthew's genealogy ends with Joseph. These subdivisions must be clearly marked before we can extract the meaning from them.

Someone once linked the four living creatures in Revelation 4 to the four Gospels. The four living creatures are the lion—the king of the beasts, the ox—the diligent servant, the face of a man, and the eagle. In the Old Testament God said that He bore the children of Israel on His wings like an eagle (Exo. 19:4; Deut. 32:11-12). Matthew portrays the Lord Jesus as the King, Mark portrays Him as the Servant, Luke portrays Him as a man, and John portrays Him as God. The four living creatures exactly match the description of the Lord in the four Gospels.

Matthew shows us the Lord Jesus as the King. Hence, in his genealogy, he specifically points out that He is the descendant of King David. Luke shows the Lord Jesus as a man. This is the reason his genealogy goes all the way back to man's first ancestor—Adam. Mark shows us the Lord Jesus as a servant, and John shows Him as the Son of God. This is the reason neither of these two books has a genealogy. When we consider the four books this way, we indeed find Matthew speaking of the Lord as the King, Mark as the Servant, Luke as a man, and John as the Son of God.

All four Gospels speak of the coming of the Lord Jesus. But the descriptions of His coming differ. Matthew says, "Behold, your King is coming to you" (21:5), Mark says that the Son of Man came to serve (10:45), Luke says that the Son of Man came to seek (19:10), and John says that the Lord came to give us life (10:10). We can find many such comparisons in the Gospels. If we spend time to study them, we will find that each Gospel has its own characteristics.

The endings of the four Gospels are very meaningful. Matthew covers the resurrection (28:6), Mark covers the ascension (16:19), Luke covers the promise of the coming of the Holy Spirit (24:49), and John covers the Lord's coming again (21:22). After the Lord Jesus resurrected, He ascended to the heavens. After the ascension, there was the coming of the Holy Spirit at Pentecost. In the future the Lord Jesus will come again. The wonderful arrangement of the four Gospels matches the order of sequence of these four events.

Matthew does not say anything about the ascension of the Lord Jesus, because it speaks of the Lord being with the disciples until the completion of the age. Mark speaks of the Lord's ascension, saying, He "sat at the right hand of God" (16:19). This is because He took the form of a slave and was obedient unto death for the accomplishment of His work. Therefore, God exalted Him to the highest. Luke records the Lord's ascension as well. God was mindful of this man, who was a little lower than the angels, in order that He would be crowned with glory and honor. The Lord Jesus ascended in the position of a man, which means that He will lead many sons into glory. John does not say anything about the Lord's ascension because it speaks of Him being our life and living within us.

Matthew's record is arranged according to dispensational truth, not according to chronology. Luke "carefully investigated all things from the first"; therefore, his record is "in an orderly fashion" (1:3). Some parts are according to chronological order, while others are according to the order of subjects. Mark and John were both written according to the order of the events themselves.

We can buy a large-size copy of the four Gospels and divide Matthew into five or ten sections. Then we can study each section carefully and consider what the other three Gospels have to say about the things recorded in each section. Similar passages should be grouped together, while dissimilar ones should be clearly marked. The dissimilar passages should have broader subdivisions, while the similar passages should have finer subdivisions. For example, the parable of the sower in Matthew 13 is also in Luke. We have to make a finer subdivision before we can identify the finer differences between the various records. We have to subdivide them in such a way that we can tell the similarities and the differences at a glance. This requires much time. It takes at least two years to go through the four Gospels. The actual copying and note-taking may only take about three months.

## XIV. CRUCIAL CHAPTERS

The Bible contains many crucial chapters, such as Genesis 2 and 3, Numbers 21, and Deuteronomy 8. Psalm 22 and Isaiah 53 are both very crucial chapters, because much is said in the New Testament about their fulfillment. Daniel 9 is also a great chapter. In the New Testament Matthew 5—7, 13, 24, and 25 are crucial chapters, as are John 14—16 and 1 Corinthians 13. In the Bible there are thirty to forty such crucial chapters, and we have to understand the meaning of each one of them.

## XV. PAST, PRESENT, AND FUTURE

This is a relatively simple method. We can group all the past events in the New Testament in one group, all the present events in another group, and all the future things in a third group. The earthly work of Christ, the coming of the Holy Spirit, and the beginning of the church belong to the first group. The Lord's supplication work, His mediatorial work, the ministry of the church, the discipline and indwelling of the Holy Spirit, and all the means of grace are things of the present. (In some cases, grace is given to us directly. In other cases, God grants grace to us through certain means, such as meeting, the breaking of bread, baptism, and the laying on of hands. God bestows grace to man not directly, but through these means. This is the reason they are called means of grace.) Resurrection, the rapture, redemption, glory, and God's new creation are things of the future. Although redemption is an event of the past, it is not fully completed. A part of it is not yet fulfilled; it will be fulfilled only with the redemption of our body. Since our fleshly body is not yet taken care of, redemption is not yet consummated. The redemption of the Lord Jesus on the cross laid a foundation. The work of redemption itself will not be complete until our body is redeemed in the future. We have to differentiate between the things that God has done, the things that He is doing, and the things that He will do.

## XVI. SALVATION, SANCTIFICATION, AND MINISTRY

Salvation is related to the life which we receive, sanctification relates to our living, and ministry relates to our work. We can group subjects such as the Lord's calling, His blood, and His work under the category of salvation; we can group all the work of the Holy Spirit under the category of sanctification; and we can group subjects such as endurance, testimony, and the power of the Holy Spirit under ministry. The Lord's cross can be grouped under salvation, our cross can be grouped under sanctification, and "the dying of Jesus" or "the killing of Jesus" can be grouped under ministry. Our faith belongs to salvation, our obedience to sanctification, and our endurance to ministry. The life given by the Holy Spirit is salvation, the work of the Holy Spirit is sanctification, and the power of the Holy Spirit is ministry. We can also use three prepositions for these three categories: *for* us, *in* us, and *through* us. Everything done for us is salvation, everything done in us is sanctification, and everything done through us is ministry. When something is done for us, we call it salvation. When something is done in us, we call it sanctification. When something is done through us we call it ministry or service. We can classify all these teachings under these categories; they can be things that God has done for us, things that He is doing in us, or things that He will do through us. Unfortunately, many people are not clear about the distinction between God for us and God in us. For example, the crucifixion of Christ and our being crucified together with Christ are things that God has done for us. But Roman Catholicism has made these items things that *God does in us*. This is wrong. The cross becomes something that is done in us when we begin to bear our own cross. We *bear* the cross; we are not crucified on the cross. We experience the bearing, but the Lord experienced the crucifying. This shows us the difference between Protestantism and Catholicism. The crucifixion spoken of in the Bible is something that God has done for us. It is not something He will do in us. Romans 6 speaks of crucifixion, Romans 8 speaks of the putting to death, while 2 Corinthians 4 speaks of the "killing." Therefore, Romans 6 is on salvation, Romans 8 is on sanctification, and 2 Corinthians 4 is on ministry. We have to be absolutely clear before the Lord that crucifixion belongs to the category of salvation; it is something that the Lord has done. We merely inherit what He has done. However, the putting to death of the cross is something that we experience. At the same time, the "killing" is the release of the Holy Spirit which is something in the realm of ministry. We should not think that these are simple classifications. Many people are not clear about their crucifixion with Christ. As a result, they are not clear about the matter of the putting to death. The fact of crucifixion is not in us, but in Christ. Everything in Christ relates to salvation, everything in us relates to sanctification, and everything that goes out through us relates to ministry. These are foundational understandings. We must all be clear about God's Word.

### XVII. MINERALS

The Bible speaks of all kinds of minerals and stones. All of them have significances, and we should spend time to study them. This does not mean that these things contain any revelation in themselves. But when God gives us revelation, He speaks to us through these materials. We must have these biblical facts in our deposit before we can put them to use at a critical juncture.

Gold signifies God's glory. Anything that is entirely of God is signified by gold. Silver signifies the Lord's redemption. The Bible does not say that we should buy anything with gold, but with silver. Silver signifies redemption. In other words, gold signifies God's person, while silver signifies His work. Gold signifies His glory, while silver signifies His redemption. Bronze signifies judgment, iron signifies human authority, and lead signifies sin. The foundation of the New Jerusalem is built with all kinds of precious stones, one of which in green in color. Green is a basic color, the color of life on earth. Hence, it refers particularly to the work of the Holy Spirit. In studying the minerals, we have to find their nature and color. Red and scarlet are two different colors. Red refers to the blood, while scarlet refers to sin. Other colors such as white, black, and purple all have particular meanings. We have to classify them and find their meaning.

## XVIII. GEOGRAPHY

The Bible contains many nations, cities, mountains, rivers, wells, etc. Everything has significance. There are the nations of Assyria, Egypt, Babylon, Greece, and Persia. There are the cities of Samaria, the city of Jerusalem, Caesarea, Sodom, Gomorrah, Babel, Ur, Shechem, Bethel, Mahanaim, Gilgal, etc. All of them have significance. Some derive their significance from the meaning of the word, while others derive it from the history associated with it. Shechem means shoulder and can signify burden, responsibility, or the act of shouldering something. This is indicated by the meaning of the word itself. In the division of the land at Joshua's time, there were many city names. All of them have spiritual meaning, and we have to find their meaning. Of course, with many biblical names we have to look in a Hebrew lexicon to find their meaning. But there are many words whose meaning is provided by the Bible itself, and even those who do not understand Hebrew can know the meaning of these names.

Under the category of mountains we have Mount Sinai, Horeb, Lebanon, Pisgah, the Mount of Olives, etc. All of them have meaning. Mount Horeb is the same as Mount Sinai. But why does the Bible say Mount Horeb sometimes and Mount Sinai at other times? We have to find out the reason for this. Then there are the valleys, such as the valley of the son of Hinnom, the valley of Jehoshaphat, etc.

There are the great river of Euphrates, the river of Egypt, the river Jordan, etc.

Many things are included under the category of geography. We have to study all the crucial items of it. However, we do not have to spend too much time on them; three or four months will be enough.

All geographical names derive their meaning from one of two sources. Either they are derived from the meaning of the words themselves, or they are derived from the history associated with them. Names like Jerusalem, Bethel, and Mahanaim derive their meaning from the words themselves. Golgotha derives its meaning partly from the word and partly from its history. Golgotha means the place of the skull. It also signifies the cross. The great river Euphrates derives its significance from the meaning of the word as well as from its history. History tells us that all attacks on Jerusalem come from the direction of the Euphrates. Even Revelation tells us this. Hence, the name signifies rebellious rule and rebellious power. Philistia signifies the devilish power of darkness. It derives its meaning from history, not from the meaning of the word. Another important name is Shiloh, because the subject of the church is very much related to Shiloh. If we would spend time to study these things, they will be useful to us in the future.

## XIX. NAMES OF PERSONS

The Bible contains many names of persons. The meanings of the main ones are explained in the Bible. It would be good to have a Greek lexicon for reference. Names like Adam, Eve, Cain, Seth, Abel, Noah, Melchisedek, Abraham, Sarah, Isaac, Jacob, Israel, Moses, Joshua, Samuel, David, Solomon, Micah, Zechariah, Peter, etc., all have meaning, and if we research a little, we will find their meaning. This is another kind of material which we have to collect at ordinary times.

## XX. CHORUSES

In the Bible we often find a passage written in a way that is different from the immediately surrounding text; the style of such passages in Greek is different from the rest of the surrounding text, and it more closely resembles poetry rather than prose. Such passages are usually not long paragraphs, but one or two sentences. For lack of a better term, we call these passages "choruses." Only those who are more knowledgeable in the Greek language can discover these portions. Examples include: 1 Timothy 1:15; 3:15-16; Titus 3:4-8; Romans 10:8-10; 2 Timothy 2:11-13; Ephesians 4:8-9; 5:16; and 1 Thessalonians 4:14-17. The structure and style of these portions are in the nature of songs. (In fact, the whole of Romans 9—11 is written in this style.) When we study them, we have to realize that every portion touches one matter or one doctrine. These passages cover everything from salvation to the rapture. For the Holy Spirit to write these eight portions in the form of a song means that there must be precious significance to them.

## XXI. PRAYERS

We have Abraham's prayer for Sodom and Gomorrah, Moses' prayer for the rebellious children of Israel, David's prayers in the Psalms, Ezra's prayer in chapter nine of his book, Nehemiah's prayer in chapter nine of his book, Daniel's prayer in chapter nine of his book, the prayer the Lord taught the disciples in Matthew 6, His own prayer in John 17, Paul's prayer in Ephesians, etc. If we study these prayers one by one, we will have a good grasp of the whole subject of prayer. We will know what words a man should use when he prays to God and what words will receive an answer. Our heart before the Lord is important but so are our words. The Lord Jesus told the woman, *"Because of this word,* go. The demon has gone out of your daughter" (Mark 7:29). This shows how important the words we use in our prayer are. If our words are improper, our prayers will not be answered. Many times when we come to God, nothing happens in spite of our incessant pleading. But when just one or two words come out of our mouth, they seem to release all that we want to say, and the prayer is answered. One brother once had an inflammation in his diaphragm. A few saints were worried that it would develop into pneumonia. They prayed much but nothing availed. Later one sister prayed only one sentence: "There is no praise in hell and no thanksgiving in the grave." That did the work. That afternoon the brother rose up from his bed. Our answer to prayer is very much related to the words we use. If the words are right, we will see miracles. We have to learn to familiarize ourselves with the proper way to pray.

## XXII. DIFFICULT PASSAGES

There are a few basic principles to dealing with difficult passages in the Bible. First, we must believe that the Bible itself contains no difficulties whatsoever. If there is any difficulty, it is with our biased and misaimed understanding.

Second, in order to solve these difficulties, it is not enough to interpret according to the text alone. No portion of the Word can have its own interpretation. Whenever we encounter a difficult passage, we have to study it in conjunction with other passages before we can arrive at any conclusion. No difficult passage can be in conflict with the teachings contained in other parts of the Bible. When God wrote the Bible, He did not write one portion without regard for the other portions. If there is any conflict at all, it must be in our mind.

Third, although some words can be found only in one place, not in other places, we still have to believe them. We should not doubt God's Word simply because of our prejudice and reason.

Fourth, we have to look for evidence to solve the difficulties, that is, scriptural evidence as well as logical evidence. God's Word is absolutely logical. He can never say anything that is illogical.

Fifth, the difficulty that we are speaking of here is difficulty in interpretation and doctrine. If there are contradictions in the numbers used in the Scriptures, we should not consider them as difficulties. These may be manuscript errors.

Recently, a manuscript was discovered near Mount Sinai. It has many manuscript errors. At the time it was made, the church was under persecution, Bibles were destroyed everywhere, and it was not easy to make copies. Copying errors are unavoidable, but this does not mean that there is a problem with the inspiration itself. It is nit-picking for someone to attack the Bible on account of this kind of error.

After we have agreed on the above principles, we can group the difficult passages in the Bible together. For example, there are "the sons of God" in Genesis 6:2, "go down alive into Sheol" in Numbers 16:30, "An old man is coming up....Saul knew that it was Samuel" in 1 Samuel 28:14, "Concerning that day and hour, no one knows, not even...the Son" in Matthew 24:36, the two swords in Luke 22:38, "Whosoever sins you forgive, they are forgiven them" in John 20:23, "renew themselves again unto repentance" in Hebrews 6:6, "There no longer remains a sacrifice...for sins" in Hebrews 10:26, "The spirits in prison" in 1 Peter 3:19, and "The gospel was announced also to those who are now dead" in 1 Peter 4:6. All of these can be considered problematic passages for interpretation. Other issues such as the camel passing through the eye of a needle in Matthew 19:24 have been settled over four hundred years ago already; they no longer can be considered problematic. Paul's journey to Jerusalem in Acts 21 is also not a problem in interpretation; it is a problem related to his own action.

Following the above principles, let us deal with one specific passage in the Old Testament that poses difficulty.

Genesis 6 speaks of the sons of God. This relates quite much to the second coming of the Lord Jesus, because the Lord said, "Even as it happened in the days of Noah, so will it be also in the days of the Son of Man" (Luke 17:26). What were the days of Noah like? At that time the sons of God married the daughters of men. Many Bible expositors think that this refers to the sons of Seth marrying the daughters of Cain. Many popular versions of the Bible also interpret it this way, but this is too farfetched. When the sons of God married the daughters of men, the offspring were called nephilim. (The King James Version translated it as *giants*.

The original meaning of the word is "fallen ones.") How could Seth's sons marry Cain's daughters and bring forth nephilim? Seth was a man. So was Cain. How could their offspring be something other than ordinary humans? This interpretation is too farfetched.

Who were these sons of God? We have to look for the answer elsewhere in the Old Testament. If we look, we will find evidence that the sons of God refer to the angels. Job gives us strong proof of this. Job was written before Genesis. It is commonly acknowledged that Genesis was written at the time of Moses, while Job was written at the time of Abraham. Later books often use the terminology of earlier books. In Job 1, 2, and 38, the sons of God refer to the angels. Hence, the sons of God in Genesis 6 must refer to the angels. The Lord Jesus said, "For in the resurrection they neither marry nor are given in marriage, but are like angels in heaven" (Matt. 22:30). This does not mean that angels are *incapable* of marrying; it merely means that they *do not* marry. God forbids angels from marrying, because they are spirits. But in Genesis 3 the greatest confusion in the world occurred: the spirit of Satan entered into a lower animal—a snake. Therefore, in Genesis 3 we see a union of spirit with a lower animal. By Genesis 6 the spirits had joined themselves to men. Angels should not marry, but they married the daughters of men. The result was the nephilim. When the nephilim were produced, God had to destroy them. God wanted to have angels and men, but He did not want nephilim. He did not produce such a race. God created everything "after its kind." Yet the demons came and joined themselves to men. The result was nephilim in the world. God had to judge this severely. God later destroyed the Anakim because they were nephilim as well. Originally, the nephilim were annihilated during the flood. But in Canaan they were found again. This is the reason they had to be destroyed. God would not allow such creatures to remain on earth.

Jude 6 speaks of some angels who "did not keep their own principality but abandoned their own dwelling place." This refers to the angels who married the daughters of men. When 2 Peter 2:4 speaks of angels who sinned, it refers to the same thing.

The English translation of Genesis 6:3 is very clear: "And the Lord said, My Spirit shall not always strive with man, for that he also is flesh." The Hebrew text is clearer than the Chinese translation which drops the word *also*. In the original language the verse reads, "He also is flesh." What does *also* mean? It means another one. Suppose we say, "You eat, and I eat also." The word *also* means that there is a second one who is eating. When God said that man *also* was flesh, He meant that something else already was flesh. What other creatures could be compared with human beings? Only the angels. For man to *also* become flesh meant that the angels already were flesh. With such proof, we can say with confidence that the sons of God refer to the angels.

Of course, man had sinned by Genesis 3 already. But the sinning in Genesis 3 is different from man's becoming flesh in Genesis 6. Sinning is an act; it does not describe the nature of things. To become flesh refers to the whole being falling under the influence of flesh; it has to do with one's very nature. We must not only take note of man's fall in chapter three, but we must realize that there was a progression to man's sinfulness. With Adam, there was an act of sin. With Cain, there was the expression of his lust. By the time of the flood, sin had developed further; man had become flesh, and sinning had become a matter of habit. After man sinned, the Holy Spirit continued to wrestle with man. But when man became flesh, the wrestling ceased. Genesis 6:3 says, "My Spirit shall not always strive with man." From the time of Eden until the flood, the Holy Spirit had been striving with man. But when man indulged in lust and became flesh, the Holy Spirit no longer strove with him. We have to pay attention to this point because the Bible says, "Even as it happened in the days of Noah, so will it be also in the days of the Son of Man" (Luke 17:27). We have to deal with this issue. Prior to the coming of the days of the Son of Man, the evil spirit of Satan will once again descend upon the earth, and sinful angels will put on the flesh. Whenever these "sons of God" cause trouble, God executes severe judgment upon them. The judgment of the flood was unprecedented, and the judgment in Canaan was serious. In the days of the Son of

Man, there also will be great judgment, and the Lord will judge the angels who leave their own place.

Are the angels who leave their own place among the one third who fall in Revelation 12:4, or are they different ones? I believe they are different from the original third who fell with Satan. The first part of Jude 6 says, "And angels who did not keep their own principality but abandoned their own dwelling place." The word *principality* is translated as "original state" by Darby. It refers not only to their original place but to their original state. Originally, the angels did not marry. For them to not keep their own state means that they engaged themselves in marriage. *Principality* refers to their state, and *dwelling place* refers to their place. What has happened to these angels? The last part of verse 6 says that these angels are "kept in eternal bonds under gloom for the judgment of the great day." Verse 7 provides a further explanation of verse 6; it does not refer to something new. The grammar of Darby's and Stevens's translations indicates that verse 7 is a further explanation of verse 6. These angels are like those in "Sodom and Gomorrah and the cities around them, who in like manner with these gave themselves over to fornication and went after different flesh." They are "set forth as an example" and will undergo "the penalty of eternal fire." These verses are speaking not of the men of Sodom and Gomorrah who committed fornication but of the angels who committed fornication like the men of Sodom and Gomorrah. In fact, they were given to fornication. In other words, they did nothing except commit fornication. They forgot about everything else and only engaged in fornication. They "went after different flesh." Hence, they are "set forth as an example, undergoing the penalty of eternal fire." We can say that Jude 6 and 7 are an exposition of Genesis 6.

Let us use another difficult passage in the Bible as an illustration. John 20:23 says, "Whosoever sins you forgive, they are forgiven them." This is indeed a difficult passage. How can man have the authority to forgive other men's sins? The Roman Catholic Church used this verse as the basis for selling indulgences. Actually, this verse must be linked to the preceding verse which speaks of receiving the Holy Spirit. In other words, the Lord has given the Holy Spirit to His church so that the church, as His representative and vessel, can forgive others. We call this kind of forgiveness "instrumental forgiveness." Suppose I am preaching the gospel, and I come across a sinner. He confesses that he is a sinner and asks God for forgiveness. He weeps, cries, repents, and sincerely accepts the Lord Jesus, but he can still be ignorant of the matter of forgiveness. If someone in the church stands up and declares to him, "God has forgiven your sins," this declaration is most helpful to him. The church can decide who is qualified to be baptized and who is eligible for the Lord's table because it has received the Holy Spirit. Under the authority of the Holy Spirit, it can exercise its instrumental power to forgive or retain men's sins. The church can only forgive as it is abiding in the Holy Spirit and breathing in this Spirit. No one can forgive when he is standing in the flesh. If we realize that this forgiveness is an instrumental forgiveness, we will have no problem with this passage.

The above verses serve as two illustrations of dealing with difficult passages in the Bible. The interpretation of any difficult passage in the Bible must be supported by enough proof and must take care of the context of the passage. No one can expound out of context or be guided by prejudice.

### XXIII. BOOK BY BOOK

We can also study the Bible book by book. We can go through the Pentateuch, the books of history, the Psalms, and the books of the prophets. The content of each book should be memorized. In studying the books of the prophets, we have to find out how many of the prophets lived before the captivity and how many lived during and after the captivity. The study of the New Testament has to be conducted in the same manner. We have to know the historical part of the New Testament. We have to know the Epistles to the churches, the Epistles to individuals, and the prophecies. A child of God may not need to expound every book of the Bible, but he must at least know the contents of each book. We have to spend at least two years to get an overview of all sixty-six books of the Bible. If we want more in-depth knowledge, we have to spend five or six years. Once we become familiar with the contents of each book, we will know the nature of each book, and we will be able to relate one to the other. For example, we can link our study of the Old Testament to the books of Romans, Ephesians, and Colossians. These are basic skills, and we have to pay attention to them.

### XXIV. IN-DEPTH STUDY OF A FEW BOOKS

After we have a general grasp of all the books of the Bible, we should choose a few books and have an in-depth study of them. This requires intense research on our part.

For the Old Testament, at least we should study Genesis, Daniel, and the Song of Songs. If possible, we should add another book from the Pentateuch to this list, either Exodus, Numbers, or Leviticus. As for prophecies, we may want to add Zechariah. Isaiah surely has special value, but many of the prophecies in that book have been fulfilled already. Zechariah is like Daniel in that many of its prophecies are not yet fulfilled. This is the reason we suggest it.

For the New Testament, we have to take up four books at least: Matthew, Romans, Ephesians, and Revelation. These are the basic books. If we have time, we can also study the Gospel of John and 2 Corinthians. If we familiarize ourselves first with five or six books, and then slowly add more to the list, we will have an in-depth knowledge of ten or twenty books within ten or twenty years.

### XXV. CHRIST

Many people have said that the Bible is a book that is specifically on Christ. The purpose of the Bible is to lead men to the knowledge of Christ. Throughout the Old and the New Testament, there is a line on Christ. We can find Christ in Genesis. In 1:26 there was a meeting of the Godhead to discuss the creation of man. Verse 27 shows us how He created man and woman in His image. Since verse 26 says "Let us," verse 27 should use the pronoun *their*. Yet verse 27 uses the pronoun *his*. Clearly, *his* refers to Christ, for He is the only One in the Godhead who has an image. Therefore, in the actual creation, man was created in *His* image.

Genesis 3 speaks of the seed of the woman. Matthew 1 shows us that the son of Mary was the descendant of a woman. All the way from Genesis to Exodus, Leviticus, Numbers, and Deuteronomy, we find the Bible full of Christ. We see Christ in the story of David. We find Christ among the books of the pre-captivity prophets like Isaiah and Jonah. The books of the prophets in captivity and those who returned from captivity are also full of Christ.

We find Christ not only in the prophecies but in all of the ceremonial laws. Both Genesis and Leviticus speak of offerings. Even after the building of the temple, there were still the offerings. First, we see Christ in the offerings and sacrifices. Second, we see Christ in the laws pertaining to the cleansing of leprosy, the cleansing with the ashes of the red heifer, and the purification of the priests. Third, we see Christ in the priesthood, in the priests' garments, and in their duties performed before God. Fourth, we see Christ in all the feasts.

Many persons also typify Christ. Some typify Him explicitly. Others typify Him by correspondence. What does it mean to typify Him explicitly? The Lord Jesus said, "Behold, something more than Solomon is here" (Luke 11:31). This shows us that Solomon is a type of the Lord Jesus. The Lord also said, "For just as Jonah was in the belly of the great fish three days and three nights, so will the Son of Man be in the heart of the earth three days and three nights" (Matt. 12:40). This is an explicit statement that Jonah is a type of Christ. Galatians 3 explicitly shows that Isaac is a type of Christ. Joseph, however, is not an explicit type. Although some parts of Joseph's experience correspond to that of Christ, we cannot find one place that speaks of Joseph typifying Christ. Therefore, not only can we find persons who explicitly typify Christ, but we can find others who typify Him by correspondence. Adam, Noah, Joseph, David, and Jehoshaphat all belong to this category.

There are other types of Christ, including manna, the bronze serpent, the tabernacle, Jacob's ladder, etc. In the Old Testament Christ is also typified by the two birds, the two kings, the two priests, and the two forerunners. The two birds typify death and resurrection respectively. The two kings typify war and peace respectively. The two priests typify earthly things (Aaron) and heavenly things (Melchisedek). The two forerunners relate to the exodus from Egypt and entry into Canaan. All of these are types of Christ.

In the New Testament, we find Christ's history, teachings, miracles, and prophecies. In Acts we see His reign today. In the Epistles we see His indwelling. In Revelation we see His reign in the future. It is a good exercise to trace the line of Christ all the way from Genesis to Revelation.

### XXVI. WORD-STUDY

This is a very important way of studying the Scriptures, and its scope is quite wide. We have covered the method of studying specific subjects. Apparently, word-study is similar to the study of topics, but actually the two are quite different. The study of topics concentrates on subjects; the exact wordings of the Bible may not necessarily match the subjects exactly, but we can consider the content and the spiritual meaning of the texts, putting texts together that are similar in content and spiritual meaning. This is the meaning of studying by subjects. Word-study, however, means finding all the verses that contain a certain word and studying them together. In doing word-study, we can supplement the Bible with a concordance. The following is a suggested list of some words: 1) sin, 2) death, 3) repentance, 4) faith, 5) forgiveness, 6) reconciliation, 7) mercy, 8) grace, 9) righteousness, 10) the Law (i.e., the written ordinances), 11) laws (e.g. the law of the mind, the law of the spirit, etc.), 12) life, 13) work, 14) old, 15) new, 16) crucifixion, 17) blood, 18) salvation, 19) redemption, 20) substitution, 21) raised up, 22) son, 23) priest, 24) offering, 25) holiness, 26) love, 27) hope, 28) heart, 29) spirit, 30) light, 31) joy, 32) peace, 33) truth, 34) glory, 35) prayer, 36) blessing, 37) promise, 38) comfort, 39) food, 40) obedience, 41) suffering, 42) temptation, 43) world, 44) flesh, 45) fleshy, 46) wrath, 47) mind, 48) generation, 49) whosoever, and 50) mountain. If we wanted to add to the list, we could easily expand it three or four times. But the above list should suffice for beginners. This approach turns our attention to the meaning of the words and the frequency of their use. If we compile all the verses together and arrange them in order, we will find out what God has to say concerning these words.

For example, in studying the word *rejoice,* we can find all the verses that contain this word. We can write down various teachings related to rejoicing and group the verses accordingly. When should we rejoice? Where does our joy come from? What kind of people cannot rejoice? How can we rejoice? If we do this, we will know something about the subject of rejoicing.

Another word found in the Bible is *food.* Let us look at some of the verses where *food* is found. John 4:34 says, "My food is to do the will of Him who sent Me and to finish His work." Psalm 37:3 says, "Feed on His faithfulness." When the twelve spies returned from Canaan, they said, "All the people that we saw in it are men of great size....and we were in our own sight like grasshoppers." But Joshua and Caleb said, "Do not fear the people of the land, for they will be our bread" (Num. 13:25—14:9). If we group these portions that speak of food together, we will see three kinds of food. First, there is the food of doing the Father's will. The more we do the Father's will, the stronger we become because we have food to eat. The Lord sent the disciples for bread because He was hungry. But after the disciples returned with the food, the Lord said, "I have food to eat." The disciples asked one another, "Has anyone brought Him anything to eat?" The Lord said, "My food is to do the will of Him who sent Me and to finish His work" (John 4:32-34). This shows us that our works should not weaken us. Rather, they should strengthen us. Not only does prayer feed us, but work feeds us as well. If we serve God in His field as our Lord did, we spontaneously will be fed as we work because our food is to do the will of the Father. Second, God's faithfulness is our food. God is a faithful God, and we can feed on His faithfulness. Every time God answers our prayer, our faith becomes stronger. Every time we trust in God's leading, we are fed. The more we trust in God, the more we are satisfied and strengthened. God's faithfulness is our food. Third, even the nephilim are our food. Each nephilim we eat makes us stronger. If we eat one today, we can eat two tomorrow, and four the next day. We will become stronger and more satisfied as we eat more of them. Many people are weak because they have never overcome the nephilim in Canaan. In other words, any difficulty is God's food for us. If we do not eat it, we will become hungry. If we do eat it, we will become strong, and the trials will be behind us.

A brother once studied the word *calling*. He put several dozen verses together and grouped them into ten sections. For illustration, I will list them in the following sections:

Section One—The source of our calling:
 1. The primary source—God (1 Thes. 2:12).
 2. The intermediary source—Jesus Christ (Rom. 1:6).

Section Two—The called ones:
 1. Scope (general)—all men (1 Cor. 1:24).
 2. Scope (spiritual)—sinners (Luke 5:32).
 3. God's valuation—vessels of mercy (Rom. 9:23-24).
 4. Actual condition—not many who are wise (1 Cor. 1:26).

Section Three—The goal of our calling:
 1. Repentance (Luke 5:32).
 2. Salvation (2 Thes. 2:13-14).
 3. Peace (Col. 3:15).
 4. Light (1 Pet. 2:9).
 5. Fellowship (1 Cor. 1:9).
 6. Service (Rom. 1:1).
 7. Freedom (Gal. 5:13).
 8. Holiness (1 Cor. 1:2).
 9. Suffering (1 Pet. 2:21).
 10. Eternal life (1 Tim. 6:12).
 11. Eternal inheritance (Heb. 9:15).
 12. Eternal glory (1 Pet. 5:10).

Section Four—The principle of calling:
 1. According to God's plan (Rom. 8:28).
 2. According to God's grace (2 Tim. 1:9).
 3. Not according to man's merit (2 Tim. 1:9).

Section Five—The sphere of our calling:
  1. In the Lord (1 Cor. 7:22).
  2. In grace (Gal. 1:6).
  3. In peace (1 Cor. 7:15).
  4. In sanctification (1 Thes. 4:7).
  5. In one Body (Col. 3:15).

Section Six—The way we are called:
  1. Through the gospel (2 Thes. 2:14).
  2. Through God's grace (Gal. 1:15).
  3. Through God's glory (2 Pet. 1:3).
  4. Through the divine nature (2 Pet. 1:3).

Section Seven—The nature of our calling:
  1. Holy (2 Tim. 1:9).
  2. From above (Phil. 3:14).
  3. Heavenly (Heb. 3:1).
  4. Humble (1 Cor. 1:26).

Section Eight—The requirements for our calling:
  1. Remaining in it (1 Cor. 7:20, 24).
  2. Walking according to it (1 Cor. 7:17).
  3. Counted worthy of it (Eph. 4:1).
  4. Counted worthy of the God who calls us (1 Thes. 2:12).
  5. Being diligent (2 Pet. 1:10).

Section Nine—The encouragement of our calling:
  1. Hope (Eph. 1:18; 4:4).
  2. Reward (Phil. 3:14).

Section Ten—The guarantee of our calling:
  1. God's nature—faithfulness (1 Cor. 1:9; 1 Thes. 5:24).
  2. God's plan (Rom. 8:30).
  3. God's grace (Rom. 11:29).

All these verses contain the word *calling*. This brother compiled all these verses together and grouped them into ten sections. Once this is done, we have a clear picture of our calling. If we pick up several dozens of these terms, we will establish a foundation in the knowledge of the Bible for ourselves.

In reading Genesis we have to pay attention to the word *generation*. For example, 5:1 says, "This is the book of the generations of Adam." In reading Exodus we have to pay attention to the phrase *the Lord commanded*. In Leviticus we find the word *holy* being used frequently. In Psalms we find the expressions *Thy word, the enemies, wait,* and *selah* used quite frequently. In Proverbs we find the words *wisdom, lies, evil, sloth, pride, heart, mouth, lips,* and *eyes* used frequently. In Ecclesiastes we find the words *vanity* and *under the sun* used frequently. In Song of Songs we find the words *love* and *myrrh* used frequently. In Matthew we find the words *righteousness* and *the kingdom of the heavens* used frequently. Consider the word *mountain;* Matthew uses the word *mountain* at least eight times: 4:8; 5:1; 14:23; 15:29; 17:1; 24:3; 26:30; 28:16, and every time something significant happens. In Mark we find the word *immediately*. In Luke we find the words *the Son of Man*. In John we find the words *sent, world, Father,* and *abide*. In Acts we find the word *spirit*. In Romans we find the words *death, faith,* and *righteousness*. Galatians uses the word *love* sparingly and never speaks of *holiness* at all. Ephesians, however, uses the words *love* and *holiness* more frequently. We have to pay attention to all these facts and should not gloss over them. Sometimes the same word is used a few times within one portion or a few portions of the Word. For example, 1 Chronicles 16 and Psalm 71 use the word *continually* seven times: 1 Chronicles 16:6, 11, 37, 40; Psalm 71:3, 6, 14. Psalm 86 uses *for* eight times, Joshua 23 speaks of *Jehovah your God* thirteen times, and Ezra 7 speaks of seven things related to God (God's hand, God's law, God's house, God's will, the altar of God's house, ministers of God's house, and God's wisdom). Paul said *whatever you do* three times in his Epistles. "Whatever you do...do all things in the name of the Lord Jesus" (Col. 3:17). "Whatever you do, work from the soul as to the Lord" (3:23). "Whatever you do, do all to the glory of God" (1 Cor. 10:31). The Gospel of John together with John's Epistles speak of joy "being full" six times: John 3:29; 15:11; 16:24; 17:13; 1 John 1:4; 2 John 12. Paul's Epistles use *thanks be to God* five times: Romans 6:17; 7:25; 1 Corinthians 15:57; 2 Corinthians 2:14; 9:15. The words *overcome* in Revelation, *precious* in Peter's Epistles, and *joy* in Philippians all have very particular meanings and purposes in their usage. In reading the Bible, we have to dig out these particular words and organize them into an outline of doctrines. This will bring us great benefit.

## XXVII. DOCTRINES

There are about seven fundamental doctrines in the Bible. They are: 1) God the Father, 2) the Son of God, 3) the Holy Spirit, 4) sin, 5) redemption, 6) the Christian life and living, and 7) future events. These are all crucial doctrines. They are actually theology itself.

Concerning God the Father, we can consider His name, His heart, His nature, His attributes, His power, His authority, His relationship with the Son, His way of redemption, etc. We must also group all the related verses together.

When the Lord Jesus came to earth, He clearly proclaimed that He is the Son. Hence, for eternity the Lord Jesus is the Son. Yet His designation as the Son occurred only after His resurrection. Hebrews 1:5 says, "This day have I begotten You." This refers to the Lord's resurrection. Romans 1:4 also says, "Who was designated the Son of God in power according to the Spirit of holiness out of the resurrection of the dead."

After we are finished with the doctrines of the Father and the Son, we can go on to the doctrine of the Holy Spirit. In order to understand the Holy Spirit, at least we must know His work within man and His work outside of man. We have to distinguish clearly between the work of the Holy Spirit upon man and His work in man. If we cannot distinguish between these two, we will not have a clear understanding of the Holy Spirit.

We must also deal with the subjects of sin, redemption, the living of God's children on earth today, and the future events one by one. Almost all theologies deal with these seven things. Once we are clear about these seven things, we will have some degree of assurance concerning the fundamental teachings of the Bible.

## XXVIII. THE PROGRESSION
## OF DOCTRINES IN THE BIBLE

Every Bible reader should know one more thing: The Bible is God's revelation handed to us in many portions and in many ways (Heb. 1:1). God grants us revelation not only in many portions but in many ways, and every time He grants us a new revelation, it is more advanced than the old ones. We have to find the advance of God's truth through the Bible. This is not to say that the revelation of the Bible is incomplete. God's revelation is contained in the entire Bible and is complete. However, this revelation is progressive. In the first stage God revealed Himself a certain way. In the second stage more of His revelation was added to the first. In the next stage more revelations were added. This is true in every successive stage, all the way until completion. We cannot say that God's revelation is imperfect in any of the stages. However, when compared to the total revelation, each revelation is incomplete. God's revelation to Abraham was perfect at his time. But when we view it in the light of the total revelation today, we realize that the revelation to Abraham was not adequate. We have to learn to trace God's revelation through Adam, Noah, Abraham, the children of Israel, Moses, etc., in a full and complete way. His revelation is always progressive.

We must also learn to distinguish God's dispensational truths from His eternal truths. In the Bible some doctrines are for a certain dispensation only, while others are for all ages. Sometimes God issued a commandment in a certain dispensation, yet this commandment was not meant to last for eternity. For example, God ordered the children of Israel to kill all the Canaanites. This is a dispensational truth; it is not meant to be followed for all eternity. We have to distinguish between the dispensational truths and the eternal truths. This is very important. Some words are dispensational in nature. They are directed toward men of one age, not for men of all ages. Other words are eternal in nature; they apply to all men of all ages. In reading the Bible we have to distinguish between the dispensational truths and the eternal truths. We have to know what is applicable only to a certain age, and what is applicable to all ages. We have to make a clear distinction between the two. Otherwise, we will face many insurmountable obstacles.

Many people have the misconception that the words in the Old Testament are only for men of the Old Testament age. They consider all Old Testament words to be dispensational in nature. Other people think that all Old Testament words are for us, and they take the entire Old Testament as eternal truth. But we have to separate dispensational truths from eternal truths. If God's word to men of a certain age is applicable only to that time, it is a dispensational truth. If it is equally applicable to men of all ages, it is an eternal truth. Eternal truths are progressive. In one age God may speak only one or two words. In the next age God may speak a little more. However, we have to know that the progression of truth can only develop within the bound of the Scriptures. Doctrines that are developed apart from the Bible cannot be considered a progression of truth.

In reading Genesis we find that God is the Creator, the Ruler, the Law-giver, the Judge, and also the Redeemer. The truth about God in the Old Testament is progressive. These five aspects are adequately covered in the entire Old Testament. In Genesis we also see that man's creation was glorious and his fall was shameful. He needed salvation, he sought after God, and he tried to save himself by works. This is what the book of Genesis tells us about the doctrine of man; however, the New Testament goes into a more detailed treatment of these five truths concerning man. This is what we mean by the progression of truth.

From Adam to Samuel, we find theocracy, that is, God ruling over His people directly. From David and Solomon until the captivity to Babylon, we see monarchy, that is, God ruling over His people through kings. From the Babylonian captivity to the coming of the Lord Jesus, we have the rule of the prophets and the priests. First there was theocracy, then there was monarchy, and then the rule of the prophets and the priests. From the beginning to the end, there is a progression from outward regulations to inward regulations. Outwardly everything failed. But inwardly "righteousness" came. Thus there is a progression of truth.

In the New Testament, we see Christ clearly in the four Gospels. This is clearly an advance. We can divide the four Gospels into seven sections.

In the first section the Lord Jesus proved that He is the Messiah. This happened in Jerusalem, Judea, and Samaria and was recorded in John 1—4.

In the second section, after the attestation of the Messiah, the subject of the kingdom of the heavens was raised. Here we have the declaration of the kingdom of the heavens in Matthew 4, the content of the kingdom of the heavens in chapters five through seven, and the mystery of the kingdom of the heavens in chapter thirteen. The second section advances to the matter of the kingdom of the heavens.

In the third section there is the vindication of the person of the Son of God, beginning from the Lord's feeding of the five thousand. The Gospel of John gives a special account of this. Although other Gospels speak of this as well, John's record bears a special significance. John points out the Lord's feeding of bread to the five thousand for the purpose of proving that He is the Son of God. From this point onward, there is Peter's confession of Christ and of the Son of God in Caesarea. Then there is the Lord's transfiguration on the mount. All of these are a vindication of the person of the Lord Jesus.

In the fourth section, after the Mount of Transfiguration, the Lord turned His face toward Jerusalem. Such a Christ is now the suffering One, the One going to die (Matt. 16:21; Luke 9:51).

In the fifth section the Lord Jesus entered Jerusalem and spoke about His second coming. After this we have the Lord's prophecy on the Mount of Olives in Matthew 24—25.

In the sixth section, on the night of Passover, the Lord spoke to the disciples in the upper room about the coming of the Holy Spirit, the parable of the vine, etc. (John 14—17).

In the seventh section the resurrected Christ commissioned the disciples to preach the gospel.

In reading the Gospels we should first identify these seven sections of the history of Christ, like setting the bearing of seven mountains. Once we have done this, we will have a very clear understanding of the works and acts of the Lord Jesus.

In the book of Acts we find three crucial things: 1) the resurrection of the Lord Jesus, 2) His reigning, and 3) His forgiveness. A resurrected Lord is reigning today, and He is preaching the word of forgiveness to all men. This shows that Acts is a further advance from the Gospels.

After this there are Paul's Epistles. We have to note the order of Paul's letters in the Bible, as opposed to the chronological sequence of the writing of these letters. The chronological sequence is as follows: 1 Thessalonians, 2 Thessalonians, 1 Corinthians, 2 Corinthians, Galatians, Romans, Philemon, Colossians, Ephesians, Philippians, 1 Timothy, Titus, 2 Timothy. (If we count Hebrews as one of Paul's books, then it should be before 1 Timothy.) The Epistles of Paul can be divided into four categories:

1) 1 and 2 Thessalonians are on the Lord's coming.

2) 1 and 2 Corinthians plus Galatians are to correct the errors of the believers.

3) Romans, Philemon, Colossians, Ephesians, and Philippians are on Christ.

4) 1 and 2 Timothy and Titus are on such things as the administration and order of the church. They do not add much to the aspect of revelation. God's revelation to Paul reached its peak in Ephesians.

From the above sequence we see that the truth in the Bible is always advancing. At the time of Paul, the matter of the church was fully settled, the errors of the believers were fully corrected, the riches of the church were brought out, and the issue of Christ's return was dealt with. This is progression. The rest of the Epistles, like Hebrews, James, 1 and 2 Peter, and Jude, are of a different nature; they have their own characteristics. Some have called these the "common Epistles." Hebrews shows us the new covenant. James shows us works. First and 2 Peter show us suffering and hope. Jude shows us the preservation of the faith. These

Epistles deal with miscellaneous issues involving a Christian; they do not contribute to any advance in revelation. Finally, we have the Epistles of John and his Revelation. Here, we find John making another advance. Paul gave us truths, while John gave us theology. John specially points out the reality behind Christianity, which is the life of God. John's Epistles and his Revelation take us all the way back to God.

The truths in the Bible are always advancing. Every truth has its peak. The revelation is unveiled in one book, and then further revelations are unveiled in other books. When the progression reaches a certain book, the revelation peaks. For example, in studying the subject of righteousness, we have to start from Matthew and consider how this topic is first unveiled. (We can skip over the other three Gospels as far as this topic is concerned.) By the time we reach Romans and Galatians, the subject reaches its peak. On the subject of the church, we have to start from Matthew 16. By Ephesians the matter is fully covered. For the subject of life, we have to start from the Gospel of John. By the time we come to the Epistles of John, the subject reaches its peak, and the matter is settled.

If we take this approach book by book, we will find where a subject is first introduced, where it is developed and expanded, and where it is fully treated and settled. The interesting thing is that after a subject is settled, nothing more is covered about the subject in subsequent books. Every subject is settled in one or more books, and after it is settled, subsequent books either do not mention the subject any further, or they skim over it. No new revelation is added to the subject. By the time the whole Bible is finished, God's entire revelation reaches its peak. God's revelation is always progressive. It constantly advances to the end when everything is completed.

Therefore, in reading the Bible we must do two things. First, we must find the revelation of the Bible; that is, we have to find where a truth is first spoken of. Second, we have to find where new meanings and new revelations are added. We have to trace the truth step by step and mark these steps down. One book may give us the introduction. Another book may give us further explanation. A third book may give us some new revelation. We have to write down and compile all of these new explanations and revelations. After we have gathered all the revelations and explanations together and have done a clear analysis of them, we can give a definitive statement about that truth. This is theology. Proper theology is a study of the truths of the Bible. We can call this doctrinal theology. If we study the Bible this way, we will have a clear understanding of the truths of the Bible.

We will conclude our discussion of the ways to study the Bible here.

As a final word, I would repeat that the person who reads the Bible must be right. Otherwise, a man can go through all the twenty-eight different plans of study, but he will reap no profit. "The letter kills, but the Spirit gives life" (2 Cor. 3:6). We are not saying that a man should read the Bible only after he is fully prepared and perfected. We are saying that while he is reading the Bible, he should take care of his condition before the Lord. Our condition before the Lord must be right on the one hand, and we must be willing to spend much time in the different methods of studying the Word on the other hand. This will insure us of an abundant harvest and a rich supply.